水

世界初!! 水の 氷結 結晶写真集
The Message from Water

からの伝言

vol.2

HADO creates words
Words are the vibrations of nature
Therefore beautiful words create beautiful nature
Ugly words create ugly nature
This is the root of the Universe

D1533305

HADO creates words
Words are the vibrations of nature
Therefore beautiful words create beautiful nature
Ugly words create ugly nature
This is the root of the Universe

IHM総合研究所 所長 **江本 勝**／**IHM総合研究所**

翻訳・愛知ソニア／Sonia Aichi

波動教育社

Index
Contents

Index

表紙の写真「愛・感謝」

「愛・感謝」は結晶写真の女王様です。

The cover photograph "Love ・Thanks"

"Love ・Thanks" is the queen of crystal photographs.

は じめに

IHM総合研究所　所長　江本 勝
Masaru Emoto, Chairman of IHM General Institute

　1999年6月に発刊された『水からの伝言・1』は、2年と少し経った今も、まるで水の波紋のように七つの海を目指して静かなムーブメントを繰り広げています。それは我が日本を発信した後、スイス、ドイツ、オーストリア、イタリア、オランダ、イギリス、フランスなど、主としてヨーロッパを中心として世界の国々に、人から人へという形でいつのまにか広がってゆきました。そして私はそのあとを追ってこの1年半の間に約40回の海外講演を行うこととなりました。それは今も続いており、私に時間の余裕があれば果てしなく続くようなうれしい状況となっています。

　この本を読んで、という感想を述べたお便りを国内のみならず海外からも、もう数え切れないほど頂いております。さらにこの本をそれぞれの国の言葉で出版させて欲しいという要請も後を絶ちません。

　国内においては特に教育の現場、それは家庭内教育を含めてのことですが、さらにほとんどあらゆる種類の宗教団体から、そして多くの代替医療関係者から、絶大なる共感をいただいており、それは早く次の写真集を出してほしいという強い要望となって私どもに伝わってまいりました。この2年間、私どもはもちろんさらなる研鑽に努めており、その新たに蓄積されたデータは十分に写真集の第2弾を発表するに足る質、および量となりましたので、今回ここに自信を持ってそれを読者のみなさまに提供しようということになった次第です。

　正直いって、『水からの伝言・1』における構成のうち、文字による言霊の部分については、一番お伝えしたいことでは

あったものの、果たしてどれほどの共感を得られるものか疑心暗鬼でありました。しかし予想に反して、その部分こそが最も読者諸氏の共感を得る結果となったことは、著者としてこの上もない喜びでありました。これはここ数年来、私が個人的にひそかに胸に秘めていた、この惑星の将来に対する危機感を払拭するまでの、ポジティブなエネルギーを私に与えてくれることとなりました。

　ああ、潜在的には私と同じような考え方をしていた人がこんなにも多くいらっしゃったのだ、それがこの写真集によって、どんどん顕在化されていっているのだという波動（あらゆる物質が持つ、原子レベルでの固有の振動パターン。エネルギーの最小単位。著者は人の意識のエネルギーが基本と考えている。）を強く感じることができたのです。

　「この写真集のよいところは、ショッキングな内容であるのに著者からの押し付けがましいところがないことだ。読む人見る人がどのように感じるかが大切なことであって、それが現代人にとって必要なことでもあるのだろう」というようなコメントをある人からいただきました。まさにそれは私の意図したことでしたから、やはりこの方針でよかったのだと、安堵いたしました。

　しかしこの第2集は少し、私の主観を入れたかたちをとりました。それを参考にしながら、皆さんがどう感じられるか、それをご家庭で、お友達と、ご近所の奥様と、そして職場の僚友と、心ゆくまで語り合っていただければ、著者としての望外の喜びであります。どうぞ、波動というエネルギーの源が綾なす美しいデザインをじっくりと感じ、お楽しみください。

Foreword

Since "The Message from Water 1" which was first published in June 1999, a little more than two years have passed. Even now, like ripples through water, a quiet movement is spreading towards the seven seas. After the book started out in our native Japan it began to spread mainly via Europe to the world. As the word was passed from person to person, before we knew it the book had spread to Switzerland, Germany, Austria, Italy, Holland, the UK and France. I followed this movement and for one and a half years lectured over forty times in foreign countries. This is still carrying on and so as long as I have time I would like to continue endlessly with this fortunate situation.

I have received countless comments of appreciation about this book from readers both abroad and at home. On top of that, there are continual offers to have the book translated into various foreign languages.

Within Japan, it is the educational scene, particularly including that of family education which has responded to the book. Moreover, almost all the religious fraternities, as well as the entire alternative medical establishment, showed a tremendous response. This quickly became a strong desire to have the next book of photographs published, and they communicated that desire to me.

In these ensuing two years, I have applied myself to further research and have sufficient newly accrued data, both in quality and quantity, to be represented in this second collection of photographs. I am confident therefore, under these circumstances, in providing readers with this collection.

To be honest, whilst organizing the first book it was "Kototama", the spirit of words, based on written characters that I most wished to communicate. However, I had grave doubts over how much of a response I would receive. But contrary to expectations, it was precisely that part which elicited the greatest response from each reader, and so as the author, this was an unsurpassable joy to me. During these few years I have secretly kept in my heart a sense of danger about the future of the planet. The above response has given me a positive energy that wipes out such feelings. I realized that so many people potentially have the same way of thinking as myself, and so I was able to strongly feel the HADO (the intrinsic vibrational pattern at the atomic level that is in all matter. The smallest unit of energy. The author believes the energy of human consciousness is its basis.) of this being rapidly actualised through the photographic collection in this book.

"What is great about this photo collection is that, in spite of the content being shocking, the author doesn't force anything on you. How those reading and looking at the book feel is what is important, and for modern people it is that feeling which is necessary", was the comment I received from one person. Because that is exactly what I had intended, I was relieved that course had worked out after all. For that reason in this second book I have limited myself to expressing what I sensed. How do you, the readers feel about it? It will be a joy greater than my expectations as the author if you, as families, as friends, as neighbouring wives or as work colleagues talk about this book to your hearts' content.

Please enjoy and fully feel these beautiful designs from that source of energy we call HADO.

第1章

ママの身のまわりで

　言葉を見せたり、音楽を聞かせたりした結晶写真など、言葉・言霊のすばらしさに魅せられた私は、『水からの伝言・1』の出版を期に、請われるままに世界中に出向いてセミナーを催しています。

　そんな毎日のなかで、諸外国のみなさまが一番関心をもたれるのは、言葉に対する水の反応についてです。これはとても意外でした。みなさまにスライドをお見せしながら、水道水、雨水、川の水、音楽、とお知らせして、恐る恐る「言葉を水に見せましたら……」と切り出します。
すると、これまでの説明にも増して「おぉ！」という声が上がるわけで、この声を聞いて、説明する私の方も「おぉ!!」と感動します。

　大宇宙の基本は、家族社会です。
宇宙社会は体験できなくても、家族社会を体験すれば同じことですね。
家庭の中のいろいろなことを「お水さん」に聞いてみました。

　夫婦愛、出産、子育て、嫁姑などの結晶をお楽しみください。

Chapter 1　Around mum
I have been giving lectures around the world upon request, since publishing "The Message from Water 1".
There is a fascination for me in the crystal photographs of water to which music has been played and words shown, expressing the wonder of KOTOTAMA (spirit of words).

As I continued this in each country, it was how the water responded to words that people were most interested in. This was most unexpected. As I show everybody the slides I talk about tap water, rain water, river water, music and how reverantly words are presented to the water. Whilst explaining these, there are ever more gasps of "Wow!" from the audience and as the speaker I am moved also, finding myself saying along, "Wow!"

The basis of the great universe is familial society. Even if we can't experience universal society, we can experience familial society which is the same thing, or so we may assume.
We asked "Water" about a variety of things concerning the home.

Enjoy these crystals like "love of husband and wife", "giving birth", "raising children" and "female in-laws".

Father
おとうさん

おとうさんは、男らしく、理路整然とした結晶ができました。

As for father, very manly and logically consistent crystals formed.

Father

Mother
おかあさん

おかあさんの結晶は、きめが細かく、包み込むような包容力を感じますね。

Mother's crystal is delicate and you feel wrapped up in tolerance.

Mother

9

夫婦愛

The love of husband and
wife

The love of husband and wife

夫婦愛

どっしりかまえて大きく手をひろげ、包み込むような結晶。
一般的には、その大きな結晶が夫で、これに甘えるように抱きかかえられている小さな結晶が妻で
しょうか（でも私たち夫婦−著者−の場合は逆のようです）。
さてあなたの場合は……？

The crystal assumes a massive pose and as if spreading wide the hands, it seems to embrace.
Generally speaking, the larger crystal is the husband, and the smaller one which seems to be sweetly
embraced is the wife. (But in our case 'author' as husband and wife, it is the other way around.)
Well now, in your case how do you see it...?

10

Mother's cooking
おふくろの味

Mother's cooking

整然とした、美しい結晶が撮れました。理由はまだよくわかりません。
普通この言葉は、個人個人の記憶の中にあって、それぞれ違うはずなのに、
50個のシャーレから撮れた結晶は、このように美しいものがほとんどでした。
この言葉は、だれの心にも美しく整ったイメージとして残っているものなのでしょうね。

A coherent and beautiful crystal was achieved but we still do not understand why.
Ordinarily, every individual has the above expression in their memory but for each person it should be
different. However, in crystals taken from fifty petri dishes almost all of them were beautiful ones like this.
Could it be that this expression stays in everyone's heart as something beautiful and coherent?

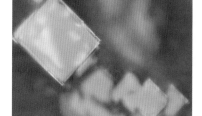
インスタント食品／Instant food

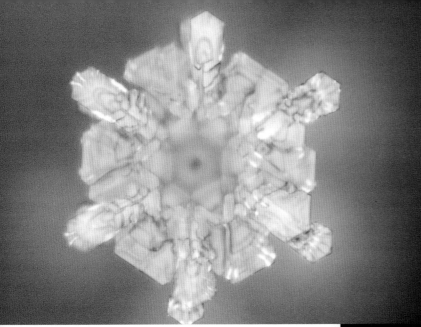

Mother's healing hands
母の手当て

全体的にうっすらとピンクがかっていますね。ふしぎと多くの結晶が淡いピンク色を見せてくれました。カラーの専門家によるとピンクは、やさしさ、愛情、生命力を活性化させたいというエネルギーをもっているそうです。

Overall, this one was faintly pink. Strangely, many of the crystals showed a pale pink colour.
According to colour specialists, pink seems to have the energy of kindness, love and an energy which desires to activate the life force.

１枚は「おふくろの味」と共通していると思えるくらいよく似ているものでした。▶

One of these was so similar to "mother's cooking" that we thought there must be a common thread.

Mother's healing hands

Female in-laws
嫁姑

家にいる女、古い女と書くせいか、少しネガティブな
結晶になってしまいました。
このような形をしていますから、なかなか仲良く……
というふうにはいかないのかもしれませんね。

In Chinese characters, "in-laws" are written as woman at
home and old woman. Probably this is the reason why it
became a slightly negative-looking crystal.
Because the crystal's shape is like this, it suggests that it
may not be that easy to keep on good terms with each
other ....
Note* In Japan, it seems uncommon for mothers and
daughters in-law to get along.

Female in-laws

Inventing new words
女へんに誉・秀

そこで私は思いついて、誉れある女性、秀でた
女性というふうに、新しい文字をつくってみま
した。
水も「そのとおり」「こっちがいいね」なんて
応えてくれたようです。

From the above crystal, I got the idea to invent new
words like a word with the Chinese
character for 'woman' on the left and with
'honour' then, 'excel' on its right. Water responded
as if saying "That's right", "This one is good, don't
you think?"

The Chinese character for 'woman'
(on both the left sides) with honour and
excel (respectively, on the right sides)

Oxygen added to the amniotic fluid

羊水に酸素

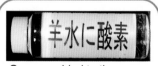

Oxygen added to the
amniotic fluid

最近、羊水の汚れがアトピーなどの原因になる……との説もあり、いろいろ問題になっています。
著書『大断言』でおなじみの塩谷信男医師（明治35年生まれ・東大医学部卒）の説によると、羊水
の中の酸素の絶対量が不足しているとも。「羊水に酸素」という言葉で、よみがえったような結晶が
とれました。

Lately, dirty amniotic fluid causing atopic dermatitis and so on is causing a lot of problems. According to the
theory of Dr. Nobuo Shioya (Physician, born in1902, graduated from Tokyo University Medical department),
famous for "The Grand Declaration", the required amount of oxygen in amniotic fluid is said to be
insufficient. With the words "Oxygen added to the amniotic fluid", we got a picture of the crystal that looks
like it came back to life.

Umbilical chord・A happy home

へその緒・一家団欒

とてもよく似た結晶になりました。これが本当の家族ということでしょうか。

へその緒と一家団欒のキーワードは、『糸』という文字。あなたと私が結ばれている赤い糸。養子であろうと、義理の仲であろうと、赤い糸で結ばれていればみんな家族なんですね。

They turned out to be very similar crystals. Is this supposed to mean a real family? The common link in the Japanese words for "Umbilical chord" and "A happy home" is the Chinese character for 'thread'. It is the red thread that unites you and I. (This previous sentence refers to a Japanese expression for a strong bond.) Even if you are an adopted child or an in-law, only if you are tied together with a red thread are you all family members.

一家団欒／A happy home

へその緒／Umbilical chord

Umbilical chord

A happy home

Giving birth

Giving birth
出産

男性からみれば、ただ「産む」……と言えるような、単純なものではないことがよく分かります。
緻密にからみあって、組み合わさり、まるで人生の根株のようでもあり、これから人生を組みひも
のように編んでいくぞ……という決心のようなものを感じます。

We can see here that it's not just a simple matter of 'birthing' as is often men's point of view.
There is a feeling here of a decision, beginning now to braid and weave life together....delicately
intertwined, knitted together, almost like the origin of life.

Mother's milk

母乳

結晶写真を撮るとき、直径1.5cmの半円錐状に凍結したその先端に、まるで母親の乳首の形をしたような小さな突起があります。実は結晶はそこを通じてからしか捕らえることができません。私はこのことをとても不思議に思っており、まだどうしてなのか分かりません。しかしこれは乳飲み子に対する母の乳首の関係と言えるかもしれません。

子どもは母の乳首を通じて、栄養だけでなくいろいろな情報もまた受け取っているのでしょう。とすれば乳を与えている間の母親は、栄養だけでなく情操の面においてもケアが必要ということになりますね。でもこの結晶から見る限りでは、あまり十分ではないようです。

When we took the crystal photograph, on the frozen 1.5 centimetre wide, semi-circular mass, there was a small protruberance. It is in fact possible to get a crystal only through this protruberance. I still do not understand this and find it very puzzling.However, we could say that this represents the relationship between a mother's nipple and the suckling baby. Perhaps babies receive not only nutrition from their mother's breast but also a variety of information, too. If that is the case then mothers must be careful during the period of breastfeeding, not only of nutrition, but of their feelings too.

Mother's milk

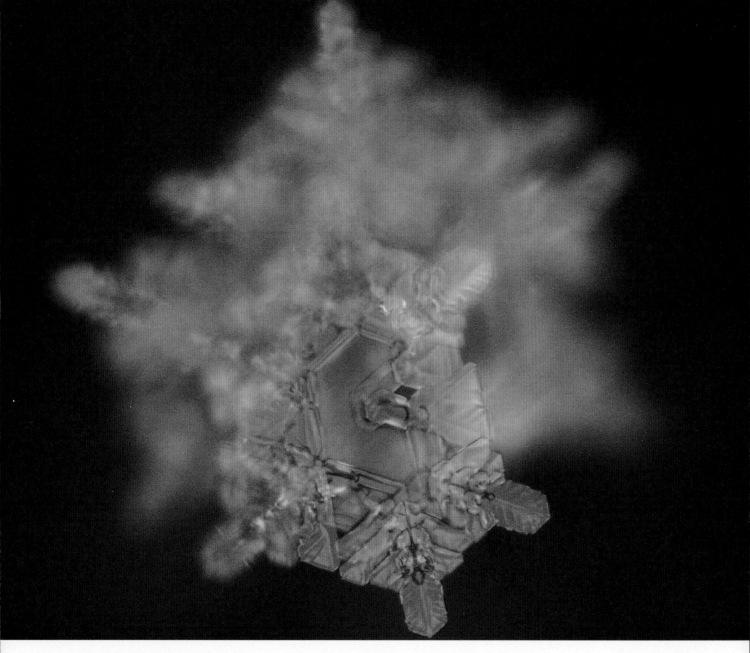

子育て

Raising children

母と子の姿を表しているようで、夫婦愛とよく似ていますね。
人間同士の育み合いということでしょうか。
子どもは、背後にあるサンプル、両親のように成長していくのですね。

It expresses the form of mother and child and closely resembles "The love of husband and wife" crystal, doesn't it?
Does this mean we humans are co-fostering each other?
The child, just like the background crystal, will grow up to be like its parents.

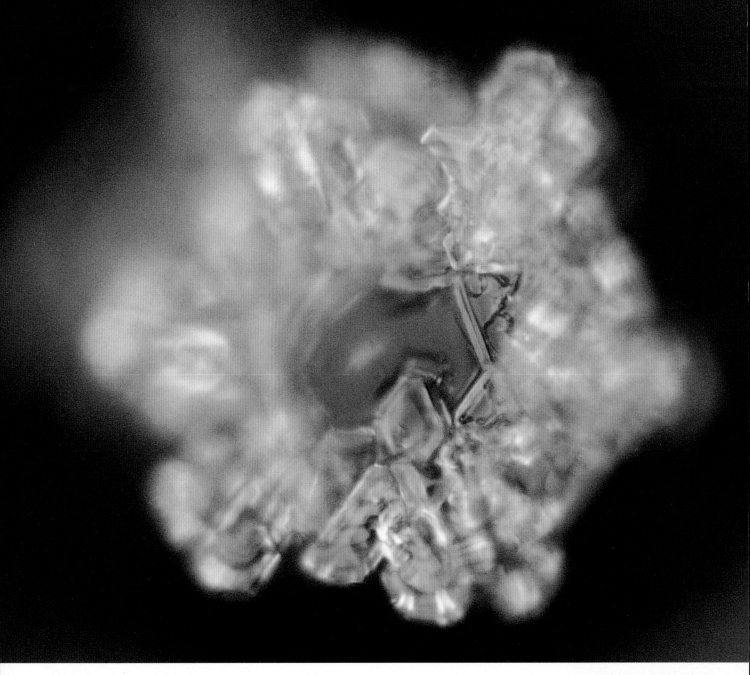

I'm sorry
ごめんなさい

I'm sorry

（株）シャープの元副社長の佐々木正先生から聞いたところによると、マナーの悪い子どもたちに堂々と注意をしよう。しかし、先に「ごめんなさい」と言おう……と、仲間で話し合ったとか。たとえば「ごめんなさい。でも騒いではいけないよ」というふうに。そうすると子どもたちは素直に聞いてくれるそうです。そういえば、日本語の感謝の謝は、謝るという意味ですね。

According to what I heard from Tadashi Sasaki (The ex-vice president of Sharp Corp.), if you find bad mannered children, admonish them in a dignified manner. "However, let's say 'sorry' first ..." This is how he apparently conversed with colleagues. For example, "Sorry, would you mind not making such a noise." He commented that children seem to listen more compliantly. When you look at the second part of the Japanese character for 'gratitude' it means to apologize.

安心

Peace of mind

不安や恐怖は、すべてのネガティブな感情のもとですね。
この2つの思いが病いをつくり、争いをつくります。ですから、この世の中で一番大切な言葉は
「安心」です。安心のできる生活、職場、教育、環境、安心できる老後が必要です。そして、この世
の中で一番安心のできる食べもの、それは「おふくろの味」です。11ページの「おふくろの味」の
結晶に似ているのは、そのせいでしょうか。

Anxiety and fear are the essence of all the negative emotions. These two emotions create illness and
conflicts. Therefore, the most important words in the world are "Peace of mind". It is important to have
peace of mind in your livelihood, place of work, education and environment. You need peace of mind in your
old age. The food that gives you most peace of mind in this world is "Mother's cooking". For that reason this
crystal resembles the crystal for "Mother's cooking" on Page11.

第2章

パパの身のまわりで

　この章は社会生活に関する、おとうさんを中心とした話題を集めてみました。

職場で必死に働くおとうさん。

家庭でも父親として役割をこなすパパ。

家族と、そしてオヤジさんを取りまく状況を水に聞いてみました。

不思議にも、結晶上における言葉は時代をも反映するようです。

大和魂や大黒柱のややなる弱体化をも、結晶は見せてくれました。

　また私は、競争社会というものは、良くないものだと思い続けてきました。

ところが……。「水にたずねる」と、大自然の摂理を教えてくれるということが、また理解できました。

生命力、パワーのあるものが生き残るということは、自然の摂理となっているようです。

どんな子どもも、親から守られながら育ちますが、成長すれば他との競争の中で生きていきます。

すこやかな競争、ポジティブな競争を目指しながら……。

Chapter 2　Around dad

In these pages we have gathered together topics centred on the father concerning his connection to life in society.

The father, who works all out at his place of employment.

Also as a parent of the household in his role as dad.

We checked out with water how dad is with his family and the situations surrounding him as an elderly man.

Mysteriously, the words creating crystals also seem to reflect generations.

The crystals reflect the fact that words like "Yamatodamashii" (The Japanese spirit) and "Daikokubashira"

(The breadwinner of the family) are slightly losing power with the new generation.

I have always thought that competitive society is not something good.

However... I understood by 'asking the water' that it teaches us the providence of nature.

It seems that the providence of nature allows those with life force and power to survive.

Every child is brought up while being protected by its parents but after growing up, lives in the midst of competition.

So let's aim for a healthy competition, a positive one...

Coexistence
共存

私にとっては大きな驚きでした。共存が正しくて、競争というのはとても悪いことだと思いこんでいました。ところができたのは、どちらもすばらしい結晶。

It was a big surprise for me. I had assumed that coexistence was right and competition was very bad but what resulted was that both turned out wonderful crystals.

Coexistence

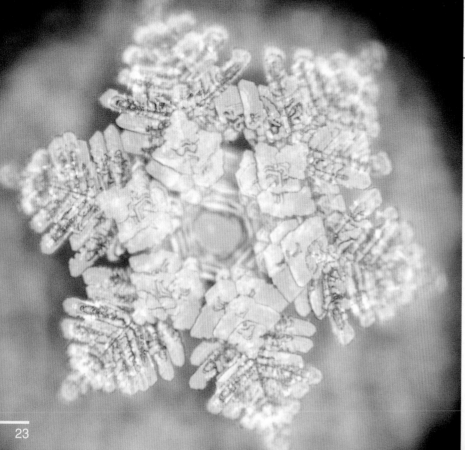

Competition
競争

大自然の摂理からみると、正当な競争は必要なことなんですね。強いものが生き残っていかないと、種族はほろびてしまうのですから……。胸に手をあてて、正々堂々と競争しましょうね。ただし、本当の弱者を思いやること、これは人間として基本的なことです。

From the point of the providence of nature, justified competition seems to be necessary. Because if the strong one doesn't survive, the whole species could be destroyed...
Let's put our hands on our chests and compete fairly and squarely.
However, let's have compassion towards the weak as this is something basic to being human.

Competition

Father's hobby
父親の趣味

私の父は碁や謡曲が趣味で、休みの日にはひとりで楽しんでいました。子ども心にもカッコイイ〜と思っていました。

My father played Go (Japanese checkers) and did Noh chanting as a hobby on holidays and used to enjoy these by himself. In my child's mind, I thought that was cool.

Father's hobby

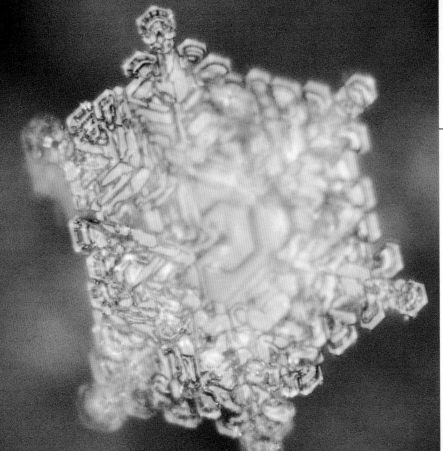

Catch ball with dad
父とキャッチボール

同時に野球も好きで、よく遊んでくれました。やはり自分にしてみれば、キャッチボールで遊んでくれる方が好きでした。そのためかキメの細かい美しい結晶ができました。
おとうさん、子どもと遊んでくださいね。

He also liked baseball and would play it with me often. Being a kid, from my point of view I preferred him to play catch ball with me. Maybe that's why a delicate, beautiful crystal was formed. Fathers, please play with your children.

Catch ball with dad

Family travel

家族旅行

Family travel

数秒ごとに成長した4枚の写真です。
家族ぐるみの行動が喜びに満たされた、楽しいエネルギーを与えてくれていますね。
次から次へと成長させてくれているようです。

Here are four photos of a crystal growing every few seconds.
We get a feeling of all the family together, full of the energy of fun and happiness in what they are doing.
They seem to suggest a process of growth from one step to the next.

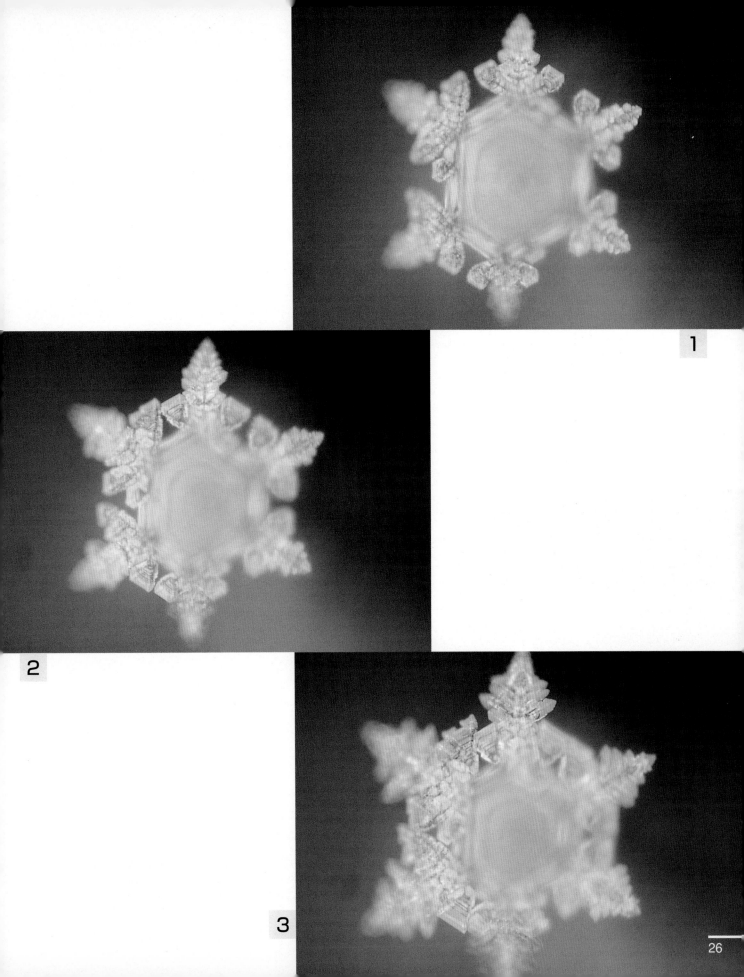

Father's teaching

父の教え

父の教えと背中、両方とも、よく似た形になりました。
背中は無言の教え。

In both "Father's teaching" and "Father's back",
the crystals appeared alike.
The back teaches without words.
(a Japanese saying)

Father's teaching

Father's back

父の背中

たとえば、具体的に父親から教えを受けたことのない人でも、父親の背中から教えを受け取るのです。
しかし、いずれも完璧な形でないのは、気になるところです。お父さんガンバレ！

For example, even people who have never been directly taught things by their father in practise can perhaps learn just from looking at his back.
However, what we find unsettling is that none formed perfectly. Dad, do your best!

Father's back

大黒柱

Daikokubashira
(The breadwinner of the family)

じつはもっと、どっしりとした大きな結晶ではないかと期待していましたが、こじんまりとした
かわいい結晶になりました。
昔のお父さんは違ったけど、今のお父さんはこんなふうなのかなぁ～と思います。
文字の結晶は、時代をも反映させて教えてくれるとしたら、すごいことですね。

I thought that this crystal would be much more bulky, but it turned into a cosy and little one. Fathers in the old days were different but nowadays could be just like this, I think. If crystals from words can even teach us through reflecting our generations, what an incredible thing it is.

Yamatodamashii (The Japanese spirit)
大和魂

Yamatodamashii
(The Japanese spirit)

骨格のいい、キメの細かい、ずっしりとして大きさにおいては申し分ありません。
この言葉が健在であることを証明してくれています。
ただし、中心の核の部分の黒い空洞が気になります。やはりこの言葉、過去のものになりつつある
のでしょうか。

This one is well-formed, delicate and has a substantiality in its satisfying large size.
That this expression is a healthy one is proven by the crystal.
However, the dark void in the centre worries us. After all, maybe this expression has a tendency to become
a thing of the past.

Letters
手紙

素朴なデザインの美しい結晶ができました。きっと手紙の方が、インターネット通信よりいいなと思っていたのですが……。しいてあげれば手紙の方が少し暖かい色調にはなっています。

A beautiful crystal with a simple design formed here. I was sure that letters were better than internet communication but... If pressed, we would say that the overall tone is a little warmer in the case of letters.

Letters

The Internet
インターネット

2つの結晶が同時に重なって成長しています。転送とか、コピーというようなイメージもありますね。でも基本的には美しい結晶になっています。真心のこもったものであれば、手紙もインターネットも同じですね。

Two crystals grew stuck on top of each other. It also seems like the image of transferring or copying. However, they are fundamentally beautiful crystals. If there is true sincerity in them, letters and the internet end up having the same effect.

The Internet

A hydroelectric power plant
水力発電所

A hydroelectric
power plant

ごらんになれば一目瞭然ですね。水は、現在のような水力発電方式だけでなく、もっと他の方法でも、自分たちを利用してほしいと訴えているように思います。

When you look at it, it is obvious. Water seems to be saying that it is not just to be used for hydraulic power as it is today, but also in many other ways, too.

A thermoelectric power plant
火力発電所

やはり大自然の摂理からは、ちょっとずれている
のかなと思います。

I think it is a little out of step, from the point of view
of the providence of nature, after all.

A thermoelectric
power plant

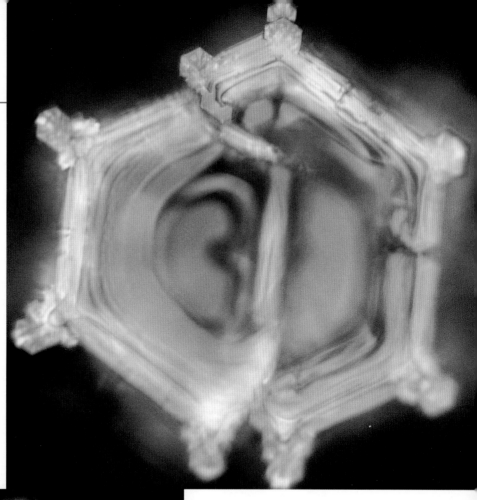

A nuclear power plant
原子力発電所

火力発電所と同じようにずれています。そして透
明な感じがします。身体の中まで入ってしまいそ
うでこわいですね。

This is out of step like the thermoelectric one and it
feels transparent, as if it will penetrate through our
bodies. It's scary isn't it.

A nuclear power plant

第3章

電磁波は怖い？

　電磁波問題はどこの国でも大きな心配のタネ。

はてさて本当に有害なのでしょうか。脳に悪い影響を及ぼすのでしょうか……。

　人の身体の中の、70％を越える水にたずねるのが一番だと思いました。

実験方法としては、蒸留水を用意しました。そして、片方はそのまま。もう一方には美しい結晶ができる

ことで知られている「愛・感謝」のシールを貼ったもの、2種類を元の水として利用しました。

この2種類をテレビに、パソコンに、携帯電話などにさらしてみました。

　私は長年、ＭＲＡ（『波動・気』を測定する器械）を使って、つまり電磁波を使って、健康相談をするとい

う仕事をしてきました。その体験からもいえることですが、電磁波は、良い仕事を喜んでやっている人に

は悪い影響はないと思うのです。イヤイヤ、生き甲斐を感じることなく使っている電磁波は人に悪影響を及

ぼすのではないでしょうか。

Chapter 3　Are electromagnetic waves scary?

The electromagnetic wave problem is a source of worry in every country.

Is it harmful? Does it have a bad effect on our brains...?

Our human body consists of more than seventy percent water, so we decided it would be best to ask water the answer to the above. As the method used in the experiments, we prepared distilled water. We then used two forms of the same original water : the water just as it was and the other labelled with "Love · Gratitude", which was already known for creating beautiful crystals. We showed these two samples to a television set, a personal computer, a cellular phone and so on.

I used to use a device called an MRA (a device which measures vibration and energy) for many years. In other words, I used electromagnetic waves in my job as a health consultant. From that experience I can also say that electromagnetic waves do not have bad effects on people who are happy working in a good job. Could it be that those people who feel neither happy, nor feel they have a life purpose and who use electromagnetic waves could get bad effects from them?

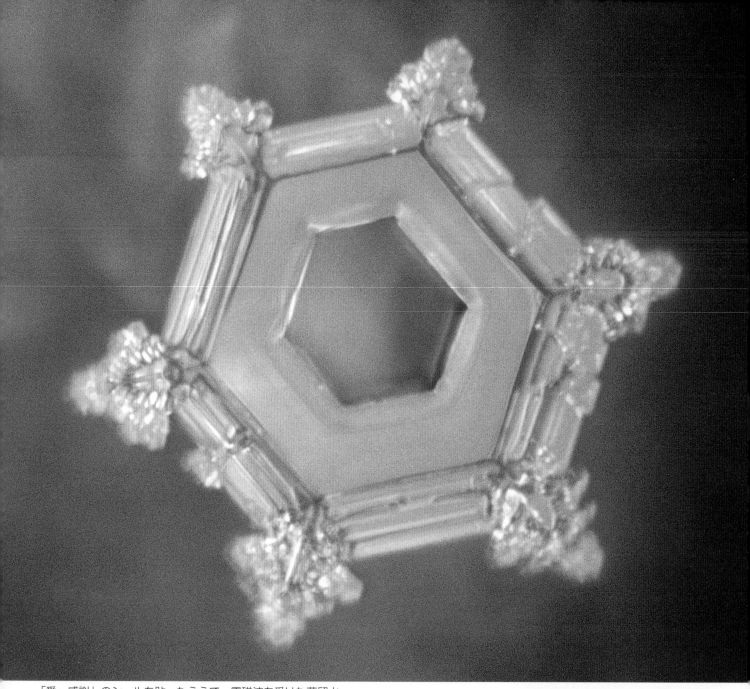

「愛・感謝」のシールを貼ったうえで、電磁波を受けた蒸留水
The distilled water labelled "Love・Gratitude"
influenced by electromagnetic waves

Television set
テレビ

テレビの電磁波を受けているところ（4時間）
The water receiving a TV's electromagnetic
waves (for 4 hours)

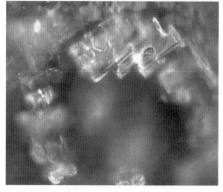

シールなしで電磁波を受けた蒸留水
Distilled water without a label, influenced by
electromagnetic waves

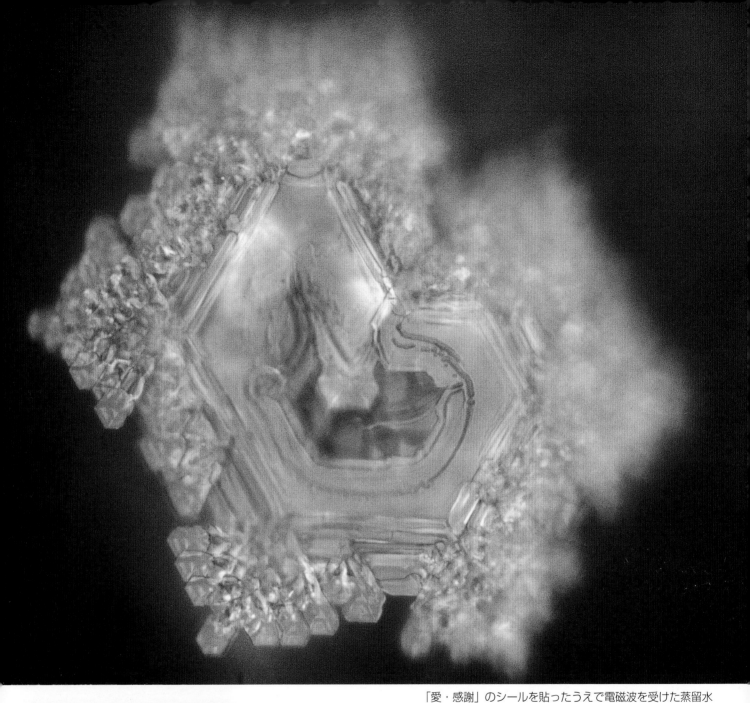

「愛・感謝」のシールを貼ったうえで電磁波を受けた蒸留水
The distilled water labelled "Love・Gratitude" influenced by of electromagnetic waves

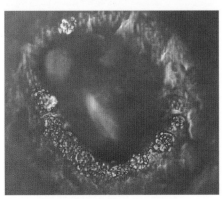

シールなしで電磁波を受けた蒸留水
Distilled water without a label, influenced by electromagnetic waves

パソコンの電磁波を受けているところ（4時間）
The water receiving a personal computer's electromagnetic waves (for 4 hours)

Personal computer
パソコン

「愛・感謝」のシールを貼ったうえで電磁波を受けた蒸留水
The distilled water labelled "Love・Gratitude"
influenced by electromagnetic waves

Cellular Phone
携帯電話

携帯電話の電磁波を受けているところ（1回1分間の無言電話を10回）
The water receiving the cellular phone's electromagnetic waves
(for a minute at a time we called ten times without speaking)

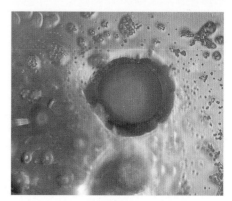

シールなしで電磁波を受けた蒸留水
Distilled water without a label, influenced by
electromagnetic waves

「愛・感謝」のシールを貼ったうえで電磁波を受けた蒸留水
The distilled water labelled "Love・Gratitude" influenced by electromagnetic waves

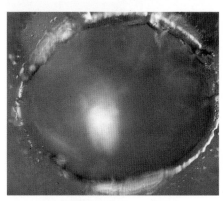

シールなしで電磁波を受けた蒸留水
Distilled water without a label, influenced by electromagnetic waves

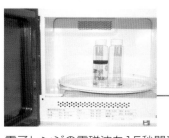

Microwave oven
電子レンジ

電子レンジの電磁波を15秒間受けているところ
The water received the microwave oven's electromagnetic waves for 15 seconds.

The distilled water which was shown the NHK video "Life"

NHKビデオ「生命」を見せた蒸留水

同じテレビを見せるにしても、番組内容によって結果が違ってくるのではというアイデアから、実験をしてみました。すると、何と「愛・感謝」のシール無しの蒸留水でも、このように美しい結晶を見せてくれたのです。

We tried an experiment based on the idea that even when shown the same TV set, differences in its programmes would change the result. In so doing, even distilled water without a "Love・Gratitude" label on it showed us this beautiful crystal.

NHK ビデオ「生命」
NHK video "LIFE"

ごらんいただいたように、この章で調べた電磁波は、シールの保護なしでダイレクトに受けた場合、蒸留水にとって好ましくないといえる反応を示しました。
結晶写真が教えてくれた、好ましくないと思われる傾向は、次のようになりました。
　　　１，電子レンジ　　２，携帯電話　　３，パソコン　　４，テレビ
　とくに携帯電話は、脳の近くで使用するもので、脳細胞水が37ページにあるような形で影響を受けるとしたら……注意が必要です。かく言う私も、携帯電話が手放せない生活をせざるをえないのですが。

　しかし「愛・感謝」というシールを貼った蒸留水については、ほとんど影響を受けませんでした。「愛・感謝」の水はすなわち免疫力がある、元気な人というふうに考えられます。いつも明るくて、「愛・感謝」の気持ちをも持った、元気な人なら電磁波の影響は受けにくいということなのでしょう。日ごろ元気な人でも、身体が不調で免疫力が下がっているときや、お年寄りや子どもは、長時間電磁波にさらされることは避けた方がいいと思います。

　特筆すべきことは、いずれも情報の内容によってポジティブに利用できるのではということです。おそらく良い音楽、良い言葉、良い番組内容であれば、便利な道具たちを味方につけることができるのでしょう。たとえば、
　　１，電子レンジ　　食物に対する「愛と感謝」をこめて調理を。
　　　　　　　　　　　たとえそれがインスタント食品であっても、「愛と感謝」を忘れずに。
　　２，携帯電話　　　良い内容の会話を。
　　３，パソコン　　　ポジティブな作業を。
　　４，テレビ　　　　前向きな番組内容のものを。
　　　　　　　　　　　　　　　　……こうすれば、いずれもよく働いてくれる便利な道具になるはずです。

As you have seen, in the case of direct influence without the protection of a label, the distilled water had a reaction that could be considered unfavourable to the electromagnetic waves checked in this chapter. The tendency which the crystal photos taught us, considered as unfavourable, came with the following:
　　1. Microwave oven　　2. Cellular phone　　3. Personal computer　　4. TV set
If cellular phones in particular which are used close to our brains affect our cerebral fluid like it has been shown on page 37, we need to pay attention. Even though I say so, I am still living a lifestyle that does not allow me to do without one.

However, the distilled water which had a "love・gratitude" label was hardly affected at all.
We can consider that "love・gratitude" water is therefore like a person who has strong immunity and is healthy.
So if a person is always bright, has a feeling of "love・gratitude" and is healthy then he or she might not be that easily affected by electromagnetic waves it appears.
People who are usually energetic but, due to poor physical condition have lowered immunity or older people, as well as children should avoid being close to electromagnetic waves for a long time, we think.

What especially needs to be written here is that each of these devices can be used positively depending on the contents of their information. If they have good music, good words and good programmes, it is possible that these convenient tools can be on your side. For example:

1. Microwave ovens	Food cooked which is imbued with "love・gratitude". Don't forget "love・gratitude" even with instant foods!
2. Cellular phones	Spoken with good conversation
3. Personal computers	Used with positive work
4. Television sets	Watched with positive programmes

　　　　　　　　　　　　　　　　Used like this any of these should work for us as convenient tools.

第4章

雨水と地震

　『水からの伝言・1』でご紹介しましたように、私たちは、97〜98年ごろ、約1年間にわたって全国の雨水を採取し、結晶を観察しました。

あれから3年たった現在、同じ地区の雨水の一部が、どのように変化したか調べてみました。

この結果、予想に反して以前よりも美しい結晶が数多く見られるようになっていました。

とくに所沢の雨水には感激するほど美結晶が目立ちました。

　その理由としては、次のようなことが考えられます。

　１，地球の環境問題にみんなが関心をもつようになった。

　２，人々の水に対する意識が変わった。

　３，結晶写真の撮影技術が向上した。

私はとくに、2が大きな理由であると考えます。

　『水からの伝言・1』を出版したことも、小さな応援になっていることを祈ります。

Chapter 4　Rain water and earthquakes
As we introduced in "The Message from Water 1", we observed crystals after collecting rain water all over Japan for about one year from '97 to '98.
Since then 3 years have passed and so we checked how part of the rain water had changed in the same area today.
As a result, we were able to see many more beautiful water crystals than before, contrary to our expectations.
Especially the rain water of Tokorozawa had such outstandingly beautiful crystals that we were deeply moved.
 The following reasons for it could be considered:

　1. People have become more interested in global environmental problems.
　2. People's consciousness about water has changed.
　3. The photographic technique used for taking crystal photos has been improved.

I particularly think that no.2 is a big reason for it.

I hope that the publication of "The Message from Water 1" was of some small help.

Biei-cho, Hokkaido
北海道　美瑛町
びえいちょう

『水からの伝言・1』では、「のどかな田園地帯に降る雨は、悲しいかな……。北海道はとくにオゾン層破壊、酸性雨の被害が大きいとされていることを立証してしまったようです」とお知らせしましたが、今回は見事です。オゾン層の破壊は修復の方向にあるのでしょうか……そうであればいいですね。

"The rain falling on a serene rural region sounds sad, doesn't it? Hokkaido seems to have suffered obvious damage caused by ozone layer depletion and acid rain." In "The Message from Water 1", we informed you of this. But this time, it is fabulous! Could the depletion of the ozone layer possibly be heading in the direction of replenishment?.... We hope so.

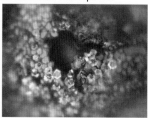

『水からの伝言・1』でご紹介したもの
The one introduced in "The Message from Water 1"

Sendai city, Miyagi prefecture
宮城県　仙台市

「杜の都」といわれる仙台の、4年前の雨水はそのおもかげを、まったく感じられないものでした。ようやくよみがえりつつある、きれいな水になりました。

The rainwater 4 years ago in a place in Sendai City known as "The grove capital" looked nothing like it does today. At last, it seems to be coming back to life. It has become clean water now.

『水からの伝言・1』でご紹介したもの
The one introduced in "The Message from Water 1"

この町ほど大きく変わった結晶はありません。
最近は他の町よりきれいです。
所沢のみなさんご苦労さまでした。おめでとう。

There is no other crystal which has changed as much as in this city.
Recently, it is more beautiful than any other city's.
Thank you, all the citizens of Tokorozawa. Congratulations!

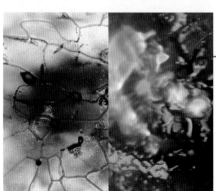

『水からの伝言・1』でご紹介したもの
The one introduced in "The Message from Water 1"

Asakusa-bashi, Tokyo
東京都台東区　浅草橋

私のオフィスのある浅草橋。問屋さんの多い下町です。最近撮った雨水は、美しい結晶になろう
と努力しています。でもまだ……。やはり車の交通量のとても多い所ですから。

Asakusa-bashi is where my office is located. It is a downtown area which is a base for many
wholesalers. The rainwater we took a picture of recently looked like it is making an effort to
become a beautiful crystal. However that is yet to be since this is a place with a very high volume
of road traffic.

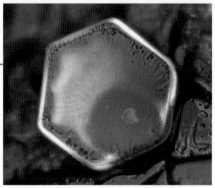

『水からの伝言・1』でご紹介したもの
The one introduced in
"The Message from Water 1"

Osaka city, Osaka prefecture
大阪府　大阪市

『水からの伝言・1』には、大阪市内のオフィス街で採取した雨水のなかで、あえて一番きれいに撮れたものをお見せしました……と書きました。今回はずっと美しい結晶が撮影できました。

In "The Message from Water 1", we wrote
　"From the rain water that was sampled from the office quarters of Osaka city, we showed the positively best shot." This time we were able to photograph a far more beautiful crystal.

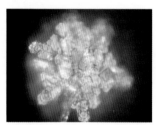

『水からの伝言・1』でご紹介したもの
The one introduced in
"The Message from Water 1"

Fukuoka city, Fukuoka prefecture
福岡県　福岡市

以前は美結晶はひとつもできませんでしたが、最近はこのように……。以前の結晶に比べて非常にクリエイティブ。生命現象にあふれています。

On the previous occasion a beautiful crystal did not form at all but recently it did like this.....
Compared to the last one, it became very creative. It is filled with phenomenal life.

『水からの伝言・1』でご紹介したもの
The one introduced in
"The Message from Water 1"

Kotohira-cho, Nakatado county, Kagawa prefecture

香川県仲多度郡　琴平町

金比羅さんで有名な琴平町は、言葉が開くという意味を示す言霊の町です。言葉が半分開いている注目の結晶です。
まだまだ、私たちの生活の中には、いい意味の言葉が足りないということなのでしょうか。

Kotohira-cho is famous for "Konpira", the guardian deity of seafarers, the Japanese Neptune. This is a town signifying "Kototama", the meaning of which indicates that words open up. This crystal is remarkable as the words seem half opened up.
Could this mean that there is a lack of words with good meanings in our daily life?

Yuni-cho, Kawabata, Hokkaido
北海道　由仁町川端

Teine-ku, Sapporo city, Hokkaido
北海道札幌市　手稲区

Iwaki City, Fukushima prefecture
福島県　いわき市

Hiroshima City, Hiroshima prefecture
広島県　広島市

阪神・淡路大震災から3ヵ月後
Three months after the Great Hanshin-Awaji Earthquake

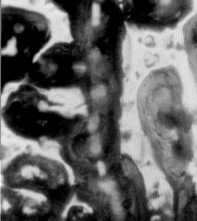

阪神・淡路大震災 直後
Right after the Great Hanshin-Awaji
Earthquake

The case of the Great Hanshin-Awaji Earthquake
阪神・淡路大震災の場合

　1995年1月17日、阪神・淡路地方を襲った大震災。その3日後、神戸で採取した水道水の結晶には、震災直後の人々の「恐怖やパニック、深い悲しみ」が色濃く映し出されていました。結晶はメチャクチャに壊れ、見る人の気持ちまでゾッとさせるような写真になっていました。あまりの悲惨さに、公開はできないと思いました。

　ところが3ヵ月後……。打ちのめされた神戸の人々に、世界中から支援の手が差し伸べられました。暴動が起きなかったことで、思いもかけず、日本人はすばらしいとさえいわれました。積み上げられたガレキのなかで、人々は人間のやさしさ、温かさを取り戻すことができた……そんな思いや願いが重なり、結晶は美しく変身してくれました。

　各地から送られてくる金品、全国から実際に駆けつけたボランティアの人たち。この「愛」に対して、3ヶ月たってようやく「感謝」の波動を感じる、気持ちのゆとりがもてたということなのでしょうか。

　地震後の衛生面から、塩素を多量に投入されたはずの水から、美しい結晶が撮れたのでした。

On January 17th, 1995, the Great Hanshin-Awaji Earthquake occurred in Kobe. Three days after we took photos of the crystals found in the tap water in Kobe, which reflected deeply the 'fear', 'panic' and 'profound sorrow' of the people immediately after the earthquake.
We felt that we could not make this public because of the horror of its extreme misery. However, three months after that.... helping hands and sympathy from all over the world were given to the people of Kobe. Also since no riots occurred, the people of Kobe were praised by many. From amongst the rubble piled up high, people were able to regain their human kindness and warmth. Since these feelings and hopes came together the crystal transformed beautifully.
Donations were sent and volunteers poured in from all over Japan. With this 'love', after three months had passed, the HADO of 'Gratitude' was able to be felt . Could this be due to the people being able to get some breathing space? For sanitation purposes after the earthquake, lots of chlorine must have been added to the tap water from which we shot the beautiful crystal photograph.

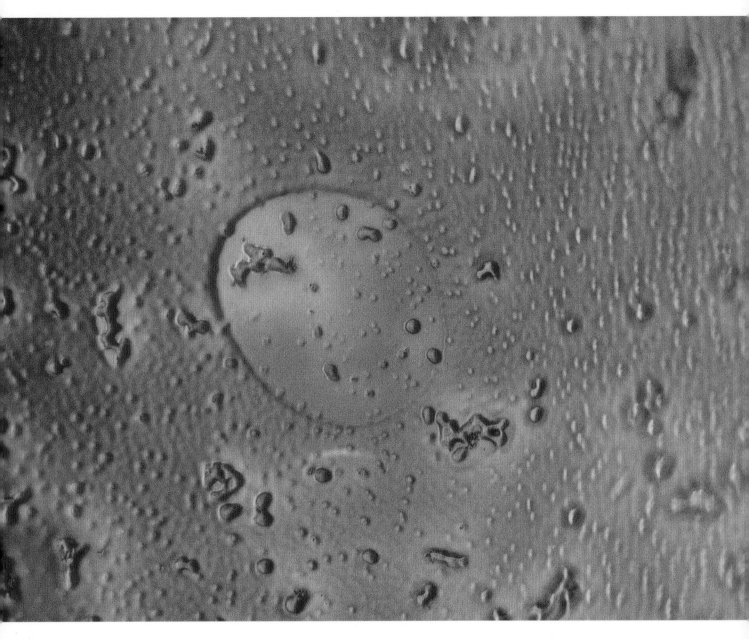

The well water right before the earthquake in the Eastern part of Shimane prefecture

島根東部地震・直前の井戸水

たまたま、島根県松江市在住の、私のセミナーの主催者である、売布神社の畑山敏子さんによって採取された、地震（2000年10月6日、マグニチュード7.3）の約7時間前の井戸水です。本来ならばもっと美しい結晶ができると思われますが、なんとも不気味なエネルギーを秘めた映像になっていました。

Ms.Toshiko Hatayama of Mefu shrine, who often hosts my seminars in Matsue city of Shimane prefecture, just happened to collect some well water approximately seven hours before the earthquake (Oct. 6, 2000. The magnitude was 7.3 on the Richter scale). We would expect a more beautiful crystal under normal conditions but it became an image which contained really weird energy.

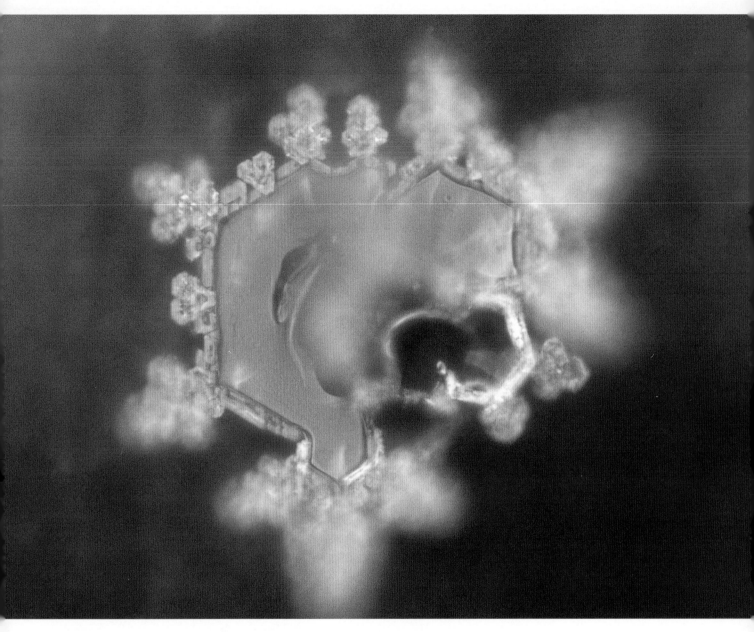

The well water right after the earthquake in the Eastern part of Shimane prefecture

島根東部地震・直後の井戸水

しかし、地震の1時間後の水は、もうしっかり復活の兆しを見せています。

However, the water an hour after the earthquake shows steady signs of recovery.

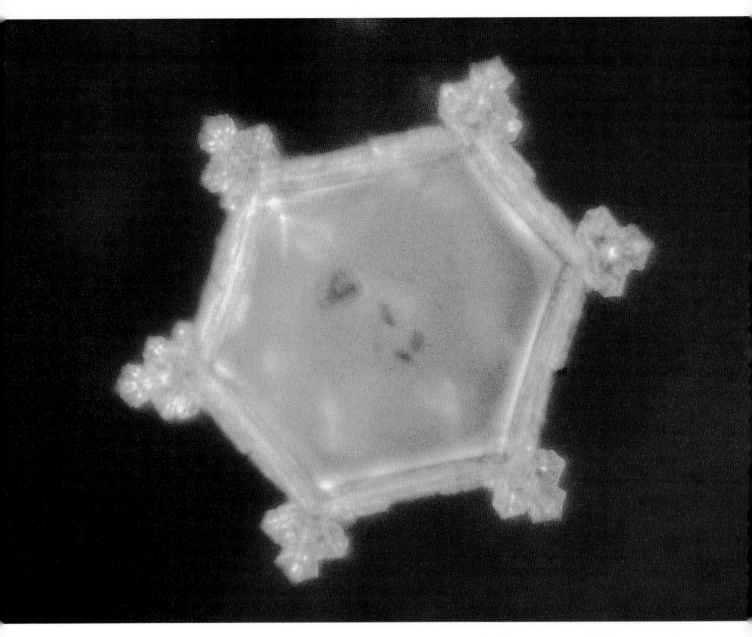

The well water the morning after the earthquake in the Eastern part of Shimane prefecture

島根東部地震・翌朝の井戸水

蓄えていた不自然なエネルギーを放出して、すっきりした顔の結晶ですね。
でも95年の阪神・淡路大震災のこと（49ページ）を考えると、水の顔の回復が早いのです。やはり一瞬にして6,432人（2001.9月現在）もの命が奪われた絶望の波動は強く、回復するのに3ヶ月もかかったということでしょうか。この実験結果から、地下水を丹念に追えば地震の予知もできる……ということを証明できた、と考えています。

The crystal seems to have a refreshed 'face' after having released the pent up unnatural energy. However, when you compare this one with the '95 Great Hanshin Earthquake (page49), the recovery of the water's face was quick. After all, the HADO of desperation from 6,432 (as of Sept. 2001) people's lives being snatched away is strong, so is that why it took 3 months to recover? From the results of this experiment, if we check the ground water carefully, we might be able to predict earthquakes.....I think that this is the proof.

第5章

水のコンサート

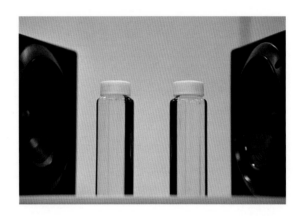

　『水からの伝言・1』で、音楽の振動を水に聞かせたときの結晶を発表したところ、世界中から大きな反響がありました。音楽ファンにとっては「なるほど……」「納得！」という思いが多かったようで、それはこの本が、そしてこの技術があっというまに広がった原因のひとつだと考えられます。

　同時にいろいろな曲を水に聞かせてみてほしいという依頼が、各方面から寄せられてきました。私たちはご要望に応えて実験を重ねました。

　どうぞ、視覚によるコンサートをお楽しみください。

Chapter 5　A concert of water
In "The Message from Water 1", we published the photographs of crystals formed when the vibration of music was played to water, and there was a large response from around the world. It seems many music fans thought, "Yes, it's true" or "That makes sense" and it can be surmised that is one of the causes of this book and its technique having spread in such a short time. At the same time requests came in from many people, asking for us to try and play a variety of melodies to water.
In response to those desires we did experiment after experiment. So please enjoy this visual concert.

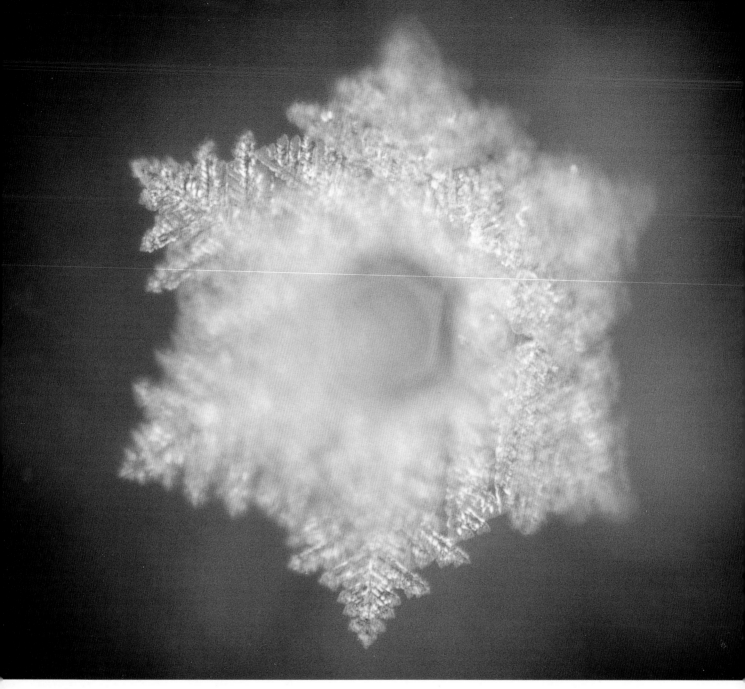

Beethoven's "Destiny"
ベートーベン 「運命」

ベートーベンの顔やこの曲の出だしからは、想像できないような結晶になりました。
でもとても、納得のできる結晶です。「運命」は全曲を通じてロマンチシズムに満ちあふれています。
私は勇気と希望、癒しのイメージを感じます。

From Beethoven's face and the beginning of this musical piece, an unimaginable crystal formed. However, it was a crystal that really made sense. Throughout all of its melodies, "Destiny" is filled with romanticism. I feel this is an image of courage, hope and healing.

Chopin's "Raindrops"

ショパン 「雨だれ」

『水からの伝言・1』でご紹介した「別れの曲」のように、ピアノ曲は結晶の粒子を細かく別れさせる傾向にあるようです。雨だれも代表の結晶のそばに、ポツン、ポツンと雨だれ模様が見えます。

Just like "Farewell song" introduced in "The Message from Water 1", it seems that piano compositions have a tendency to make the particles of a crystal finely disperse. We can also see the pattern of raindrops here and there next to the representative crystal of "Raindrops".

Tchaikovsky's "Swan Lake"
チャイコフスキー「白鳥の湖」

悪魔によって白鳥に変えられた村娘に恋をし、さまよう王子。
いかにも美しい瀕死の白鳥という感じの結晶がとれました。
そしてまた、不思議な虹の結晶や愛に包まれたような結晶も見せてくれました。

The village girl is transformed into a white swan by a demon and the prince who falls in love with her starts wandering. Here we got a crystal for sure that feels like the beautiful swan on the verge of death. Then also, a strange rainbow crystal as well as one that seems enveloped in love appeared.

Schubert's "Ave Maria"

シューベルト「アヴェマリア」

アヴェマリアという曲は何曲かありますが、私はシューベルトの曲が大好きで、『水からの伝言・1』
の読者からも、その結晶が見たいという、多数のご希望をいただきました。
予想通り、すばらしい均整のとれた、愛にあふれる結晶になりました。

There are several "Ave Maria" compositions, but I like Schubert's melody very much. From readers of "The
Message of Water 1", we received many requests to see the crystal of that piece of music.
Just as expected we got a wonderfully symmetrical crystal replete with love.

Smetana's "Moldau"
スメタナ「モルダウ」

私の知人、小林研一郎さんの指揮の曲。とても素晴らしい、人情味あふれる指揮をすることで定評のある人です。滔々（とうとう）とした、慈愛に満ちた結晶になりました。チェコスロバキアの南西部、シュマバ山脈に発し、エルベ川に流れ込む「ブルタバ川」がモルダウ川の本名。美しい音楽にふさわしく美しい水の顔を見せてくれました。

This is a piece conducted by a friend of mine, Mr. Kennichiro Kobayashi.
He is acknowledged as one who conducts with a wonderful, fine human touch. A majestic crystal, full of affection, resulted. The real name of the River Moldau, which flows into the Elbe river
starting from the Sumava mountains in south West Czechoslovakia, is the river Voltava. We are shown the beautiful face of water appropriate for such beautiful music.

ワグナー「ヴァルキューレの騎行」

すばらしい美しさの結晶ですが、真ん中がボケてしまいました。
撮影者に言わせると、とてもすばらしく整った、美しい結晶だったそうです。ところが、思ったより早いスピードで成長したために、一瞬シャッターチャンスが遅れてしまいましたが、本当は完璧な結晶だったとのことです。

Although there is wonderful beauty in this crystal, the centre is unfocussed. According to the photographer, it was a really well formed and beautiful crystal. However, because this crystal formed at a faster speed than expected, he was too late to snap the shot.
He said that otherwise it would have been a perfect crystal.

夏／Summer

春／Spring

Vivaldi's "The Four seasons" Spring, Summer, Autumn, Winter

ビヴァルディ 「四季」 春夏秋冬

春……花が芽吹いている。夏……立派に成長して、咲き誇っている。秋……実り、愛の結晶ができて、そのタネを体内に宿して。冬……じっと滋養を蓄えて熟しつつ、春を待っているようです。
こんな結晶たちにコメントをつけるのは、自分たちの子どもに名前をつけているような気がします。

Spring...Flowers are budding.
Summer...Splendidly growing, they triumphantly bloom.
Autumn...Ripening, a crystal of love is formed and its seed lives in its body.
Winter...Storing its nourishment in stillness it matures, as if waiting for Spring.
In making comments on these crystals, it feels like I am deciding on names for my children.

秋／Autumn

冬／Winter

Mendelssohn's "The wedding march"
メンデルスゾーン「結婚行進曲」

華やかな結婚行進曲を聞かせたお水の結晶です。
花嫁が最高に美しく輝いている……そういう姿がイメージされます。

Here is the crystal from water which has been played the gay wedding march melody.
It is an image like the new bride, glittering at her most beautiful.

サラサーテ「ツィゴイネルワイゼン」

情熱的なジプシーをイメージして作られたこの曲。
もっと奔放な感じの結晶をつくるかと思いましたが、意外に安定した美しい結晶となりました。
本来は、彼らも静かに憩えるところを求めているのかもしれませんね。

This piece was composed with the image of a passionate gypsy in mind. I thought this might make a crystal with a more extravagant feel to it. However, it ended up more settled and beautiful than expected. Who knows, perhaps they are originally in search of a place where they can quietly relax.

Albinoni's "Adagio from Albinoni"
アルビノーニ「アルビノーニのアダージョ」

アルビノーニは18世紀のイタリアで、オペラをたくさんつくった人。
この結晶写真は、ぜひ、この曲を実際に聞きながら見ていただきたいものです。
ロマンチックな中にも芯の強さを感じる、叙情的な曲ですが、結晶も独特な形を見せてくれました。

Albinoni is a man who composed many operas in the eighteenth century in Italy. I would very much like you to look at this crystal photograph whilst actually listening to this piece. It is a lyrical melody, yet you can feel the strength of the core within its romanticism. This crystal also displays a unique form.

ジル・パース 「Chanting Meditations」

イギリスの著名な科学者である、ルパート・シェルドレイク博士の奥さんのジル・パースさんのオーバートーンのチャンティング（泳唱）です。このチャンティングは、響きがベースとなるマントラ（祈り）に似ていて、ハーモニーが強調されるので、実際よりも大きく聞こえます。よって物質そのものの構造原理を聞くことができます。結晶がつくりだした異次元の世界。七角形を見せています。

Jill Purce is the wife of prominent British scientist Dr. Rupert Sheldrake and this is from the CD of her overtone chanting. This chanting is based on resonance, resembles mantra and amplifies the harmonics so that they are louder than the fundamental, thus enabling you to hear the very structure of matter itself. The crystal shows us a seven sided world, from a different dimension that it has created.

1.YOU INSPIRE ME（解放 ← 抑圧 副腎波動）
（Release←Supression　Adrenal HADO）

2.KEYS TO MY HEART（情熱 ← 無気力 松果体波動）
（Passion←Lethargy　Pineal HADO）

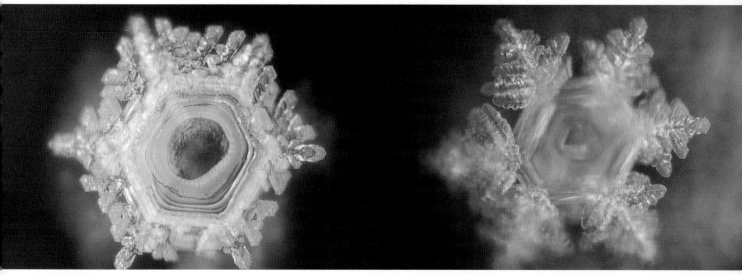

3.(THE) BOHEMIAN（やさしさ ← 寂しさ 脳波動）
（Kindness←Loneliness　Brain HADO）

4. IN THE DARK（感謝 ← 恨み 肺波動）
（Gratitude←Grudge　Lung HADO）

Alan Rubik's "Keys To My Heart"

アラン・ルービック「Keys To My Heart」

世界ではじめての結晶ＣＤ。蒸留水にこれらの曲を１曲ずつ聞かせてから、結晶を撮影した新しいタイプのヒーリングＣＤです。

そして、それぞれの結晶を波動測定器『ＭＲＡ』（『波動・気』を測定する器械）で測定したところ上記のようなコードと共鳴しました。

それぞれの曲のポジティブな感情を、イメージしながら聞いてください。

This is the first CD of crystals in the world and also a new type of healing music.

The crystal photographs were taken after playing each of these melodies to distilled water.

Then when each crystal was gauged with a HADO measuring device called an MRA (a device which measures vibration and energy) it resonated with the above types of codes. Please visualise the positive emotion of each melody while listening to them.

5. I REMEMBER（創造性　←　妄想　右脳波動）
（Creativity←Fantasy　Right brain HADO）

6. TENDERNESS（いつくしみ　←　自己憐憫　自律神経波動）
（Affection←Self-pitty　Autonomic nerve HADO）

7. NIGHT AND DAY（心の平安　←　自制心を失う恐れ　頭骸骨波動）
（Peace of mind←Fear of losing self-control　Cranial HADO）

8. ONCE MORE（幸せ　←　アンラッキー　胸腺波動）
（Happiness←Unluckiness　Thymus HADO）

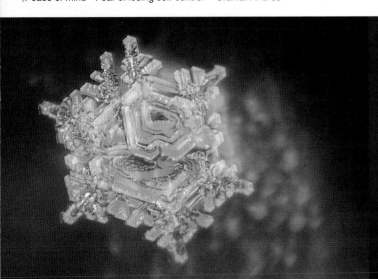

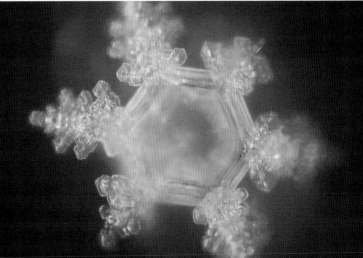

9. STARLIGHT（思いやり　←　いらだち・あせり　膵臓波動）
（Sympathy←Irritation・Impatience　Pancreatic HADO）

10. ANGEL（きずな　←　対人関係ストレス　血液循環波動）
（Bonds←Stress of human relations　Blood circulation HADO）

Bud Powell's "Cleopatra's Dream"

バド・パウエル 「Cleopatra's Dream」

6歳のころからピアノに親しみ、モダンジャズのピアノ・トリオスタイルを創った人。
結晶がこのように美しい六角形を見せるということは、モダンジャズといえども大自然のリズムに
マッチした作風であり、曲なのだと水が教えてくれています。

This is a man who grew fond of the piano at age six and later created a piano trio style for
modern jazz. That the crystal shows us this beautiful hexagonal shape teaches us that this is a piece
matching the rhythms of nature, despite its being modern jazz.

Hikaru Utada's "Automatic"

宇多田ヒカル「**Automatic**」

正直言って、私のような戦中派には「？」という感じがありますが、しかし、このようにあらわれる結晶に「なるほど、これはすごいな」と、すっかり好きになりました。
本物はやはり違うのですね。

To be honest, people from the war generation like myself probably wouldn't appreciate this music (Young Japanese pop star's song). However on seeing this kind of crystal I got to like it saying, "How about that, it's really great." The real McCoy is different from others.

Balinese Choral Drama "Kecak"
バリ島呪的合唱曲より「ケチャ」

まるでレース編みのようで、キメが細かく、大きなエネルギーをもっています。
サンスクリット語を見せた結晶（114ページ）に、とてもよく似ています。
この音楽の原点とサンスクリット語が、同じ時代のものなのかもしれませんね。

It looks just like embroidered lace, which is delicate but also possesses a strong energy.
This very much resembles the crystal (page114) that the Sanskrit language was shown to.
It could be possible that the origin of this music and Sanskrit are from the same historical period.

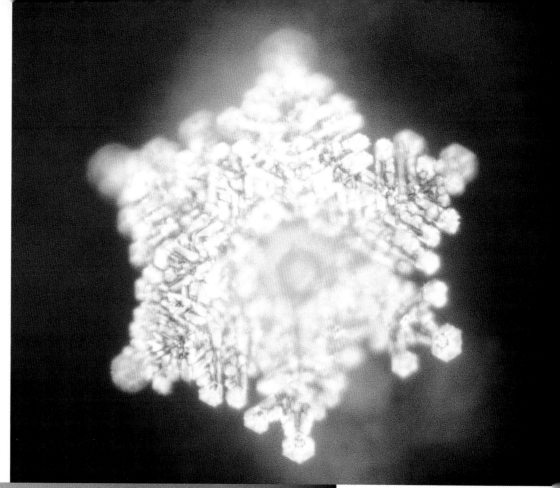

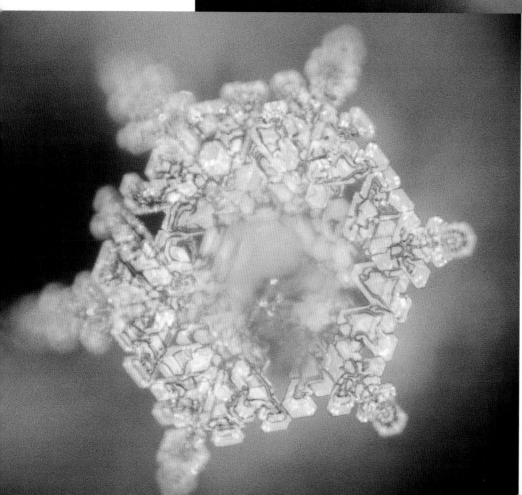

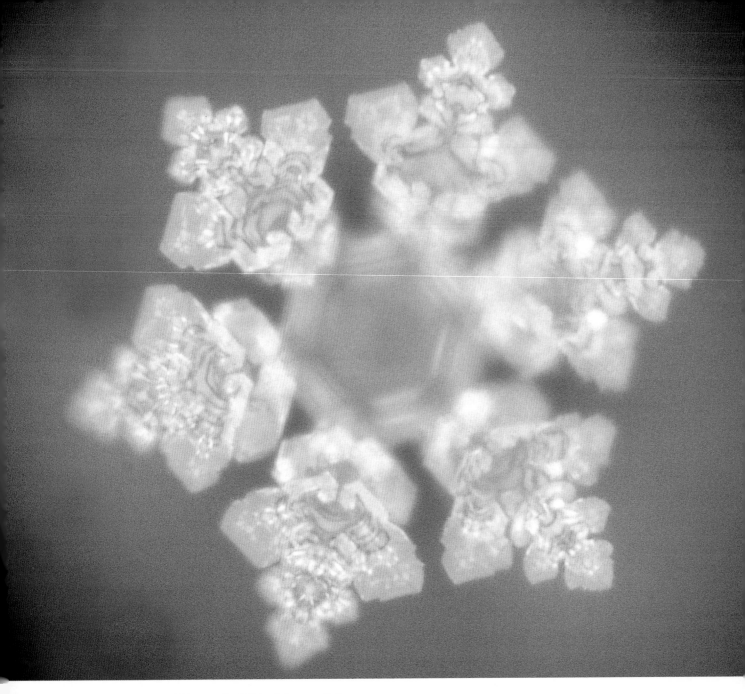

A Japanese children's song "Akatombo" (Red dragonfly)

童謡 「赤とんぼ」

夕焼けこやけの　赤とんぼ……。
赤とんぼたちが編隊を組んでねぐらに帰っていきます。
しっかりと美しい結晶を見せてくれる歌の数々は、いつまでも忘れずに歌い継ぎたいものですね。

"Red dragonfly is flying in the sunset's glow..."
The red dragonflies fly in a formation back to their nest. Solid and beautiful crystals are shown by so many songs that we would like to keep on singing them without ever forgetting.

A Japanese children's song "Chiisai aki mitsuketa" (I found a little Autumn)

童謡 「小さい秋みつけた」

小さい秋、小さい秋、小さい秋、見つけた……。
歌詞のように、小さな秋がポツンと浮かんでいます。
遠くの方にも、もっと小さな秋が浮かんでいます。

"A little autumn, a little autumn, a little autumn I found..." is how this Japanese song goes.
Just like the lyrics say, a little piece of Autumn is in the air. Also, further in the distance, an even smaller
Autumn is in the air...

1

A Japanese children's song
"Mikan no hana saku oka"
 (The hill where the tangerine blossoms bloom)

童謡 「みかんの花咲く丘」

2

1つの結晶の成長の過程で、とても美しい色を撮影することができました。
緑が少しずつ成長しながら、熟していくようすを見せてくれているようです。
みかんの花が、咲いている……。

In the process of the formation of one crystal, we were able to photograph a very beautiful colour.
As the green was growing little by little, it seems that we were being shown the ripening process.
The tangerine flowers, they were blossoming....

3

4

78

第6章

水も楽しんでます

　この章では、日本古来の伝統音楽や芸能を聞かせたり、いろいろな写真を見せて、水の反応をみました。ごらんのように、それぞれの試みに水は素直に応えてくれました。水自体も楽しみながら、私たちに何かを伝えようとしています。

　これらはまだ、根拠のあることとしては理解できませんが、私個人の感覚としては、それぞれに感じるものがありました。水が伝えていることを私なりに感じて私なりに表現しました。
　読者のみなさんもそれぞれに感じ、また楽しんでくだされば、こんなにうれしいことはありません。

Chapter 6　Water is also having fun
In this chapter, we look at the reaction of water, when being shown different photographs and being played ancient Japanese traditional music and performing arts. Each time we attempted this, the water responded frankly. Water is attempting to communicate something to us whilst at the same time enjoying itself.

These things can not be understood yet under any basis but as for my feeling as an individual, each and every image had something I could sense. I have expressed in my own way what I felt that water wanted to express. What would make me most happy is if each reader sensed each one in his or her own way and had a lot of fun doing it.

Koto (Japanese harp) "Rokudan" (sixth level)
琴「六段」

琴という振動の響きの代表のような、和楽器の奏でる曲。まさに振動がうみ出す音楽の結晶です。13本の弦がかもし出す独特の振動が、美しい六角形をつくりました。

力強く、また軽やかに、そして厳かな振動のぶつかり合いは、響き合い、重なり合っているような紋様を見せてくれたようです。

This is a piece played on a Japanese instrument representing the resonant vibration of the Koto. The crystal is exactly like music created by vibration. The thirteen strings which engender this unique vibration formed a hexagonal crystal.

It seems to be showing us a collision of powerful and also light vibrations which resonate together and pile upon each other.

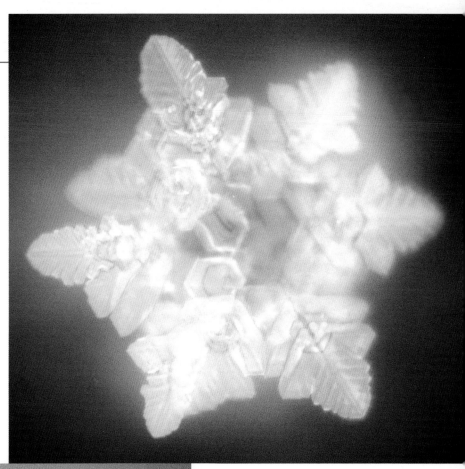

Gagaku (Imperial court music) "Hyochou-etenraku"
雅楽「平調越天楽」

唐楽の小曲。私の高校時代の音楽の教科書にありました。

この題名から想像するとしたら、天国を越えて、さらに楽しいところ……ということでしょうか。確かにそのような結晶になりましたね。

This is a short Tang dynasty composition. It was in my high school music textbook.

If you imagined something based on the characters in the title it might be that of going beyond heaven to an even more joyful place.

It became a crystal which certainly looks like that.

Kouta (Ballad) "Tsurukame" (Crane and Turtle...
often sung at joyful occasions like weddings)

小唄 「鶴亀」

今回の撮影では、どうやら鶴さんより亀さんの
方が浮かび上がって見えるようです。ちょっと
華奢な亀さんですね。鶴さんに影響をもたらさ
れているようです。

During the photographing of this, it seems that Mr.
Turtle is more visible than Mr. Crane. He seems to
be a rather slender turtle, doesn't he? Perhaps he
is being influenced by Mr. Crane...

Nagauta (Shamisen accompanied song)
"Matsu no Midori" (Green of the Pine)

長唄 「松の緑」

この曲は、華やかな遊女の姿など、廓の気分を
謡っているとのことです。美しい結晶ですが、
中心の核の部分のグレイの空洞が気になります。

This is a song about the feelings of the gay
quarters and their gorgeous courtesans there. It is
a beautiful crystal, but the grey void at the central
core is a little unsettling...

Folk song "Miyakejima no Doutsuki Uta" (Miyake Island's pounding the ground song)

民謡「三宅島のどうつき唄」

この曲をみんなで謡うことによって、身体の中の水分がリラックスし、持てる力が最大限に発揮できるのでしょう。
三宅島のみなさん、この歌を謡いながら、1日も早く島に帰ることができる日をイメージし、楽しみにしてください。

By all singing this song together, the water in our bodies relaxes and the energy we have will be activated to the fullest. People of Miyake Island (which was evacuated due to a volcanic eruption there in 2000), while you sing this song, please look forward to the day when you will be able to return to your island without delay.

Folk Song "Mogami-gawa Funauta"
(The Mogami river boat song)

民謡 「最上川舟唄」

♪酒田さ行くはげ、達者でろちゃ～
流行風邪などひがねよに……♪
と謡われる最上川は、富士川、球磨川とともに、
日本3急流のひとつ。
舟をこぐ船頭さんは急流ではかけ声を交わし合
い、ゆったりとした下流では、この歌を謡いなが
ら、川を下っていったのでしょうか。

This song is about the Mogami river, one of the
three fastest flowing rivers in Japan along with the
Fuji and Kuma rivers. Going down river in the old
days, the boat leader who was on the oar would
shout out over the rapids and when the current
slowed down, maybe he would sing this song as
they carried on downstream.

Folk song "Tsugaru no Komori-uta"
(The babysitter in Tsugaru song)

民謡 「津軽の子守り唄」

結晶の背後に「わたあめ」のような、いくつかの結晶
が見えます。本体の結晶も少しボケていますが、まる
でなにか大切なものを抱っこしているようにも見えませ
んか。

In the background of the large crystal, you can see
several ones that look like candyfloss. The main body
itself is a little fuzzy and doesn't it look almost as if it were
embracing something important?

'Rakugo' (traditional style comic story) "Yabuiri" by Kinba Sanyutei

落語 三遊亭金馬 「藪入り」

なぜ落語を聞くと、人々は楽しくなり、笑い出すのでしょう。
水に落語を聞かせてみると、ごらんのようにさまざまな結晶ができました。きっと水も、話の内容から、さまざまな喜怒哀楽を感じ取ったに違いありません。
「おあとが、よろしいようで……」とでも言いたげに、後ろにも結晶が控えているものもあります。

Why is it that when people listen to Rakugo they have such fun and burst out laughing? As you can see here when we let the water hear Rakugo, there was this variety of crystals. The water must also have felt a variety of emotions, of joy and anger, from the contents of the story.
"Well, here comes the next......" (a traditional ending in Rakugo) seems to be what the crystal in the background is saying.

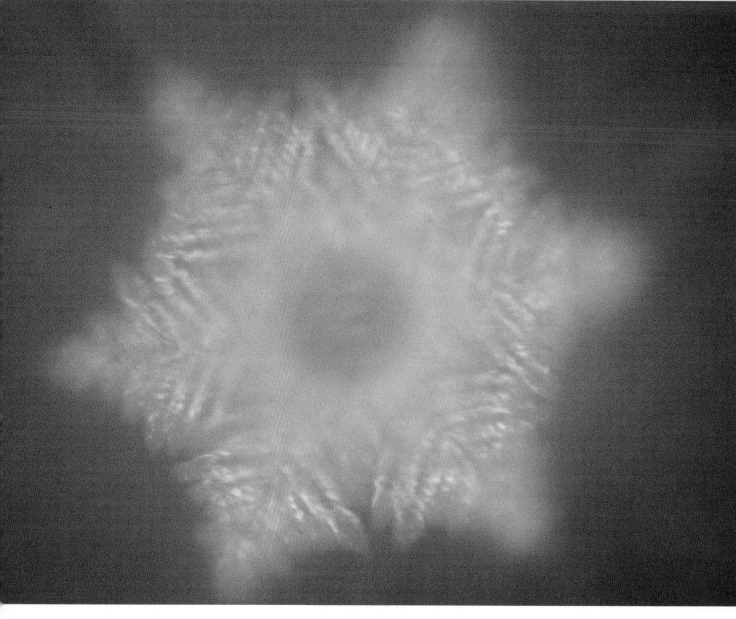

Environmental music "Yoru no mori no oto" (The sounds of the night forest)

環境音楽 「夜の森の音」

この1枚に代表されるように、50個のシャーレのほとんどから、暗闇にぼんやり……の結晶ばかり
ができました。これは、どんなに暗い夜にも「音＝光」があるということを表しているようです。
だから音という文字をもんがまえで閉じこめて、闇という文字になるのでしょうね。
暗いから闇ではなくて、音がないから闇なのです。

What is represented in this one shot is like the crystals that formed in almost all the 50 petri dishes.The
crystals were in darkness and indistinct meaning that no matter how dark the night, where there is sound
there is light. That's why if you enclose the character for 'sound' inside of the one for 'gate', you end up with
'darkness'. It is not dark because of darkness itself, it is dark because there is no sound.

これまでは水に音楽などを聞かせて結晶をみてきましたが、今度は写真の上に水を置いて、
写真の持っている情報を水がどのようにとらえるかの実験をしてみました。

We have seen crystals that have been played music and other sounds until now but these next ones are of water that has been placed on top of photographs. We tried in these experiments to find out how water would react to the information in the photographs.

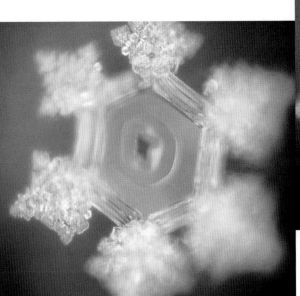

Water that was shown a photograph of Jomon cedar trees

「縄文杉」の写真

この結晶は成長の課程で、およそ数秒ごとにゆっくりと、淡いピンクとブルーの発色ををくり返しました。縄文杉が6千年たっても、しっかりとした良い呼吸をしているためかと考えられます。それが「長生・長息(ながいき)」のヒミツなのかもしれませんね。

Within the process of this crystal forming, during the few seconds of shooting, light pink and blue colours appeared repeatedly. It can be surmised that, even if a Jomon cedar is six thousand years old, it has steady, good breathing. This might be the secret of long life.

Water that was shown a photograph of a lotus flower

3

「蓮の花」の写真

蓮の花と言えばお釈迦様。
お釈迦様は、汚泥の中から美しい花を咲かせる蓮のように「たとえ今、泥沼の中にいたとしても、それに染まらずに、だれでもみんなが美しい花を咲かせることができるんだよ」と教えています。
1, 2, 3と成長していく結晶です。六角形の原型に6つ以上の枝をつけているうえに、裏のもう1つの結晶が同時に成長していて、蓮の花のエネルギーを感じます。

The lotus flower reminds us of the Buddha. The Buddha teaches us, just like the beautiful lotus flower that blooms out of dirty swamps. "Even if you were now in a dirty swamp, you should not be influenced, so every single one of us can bloom like a beautiful flower." You can see the crystal growing in photos 1, 2 and 3. On top of the archetypal hexagon's six sides, this crystal forms other branches. Besides that, another crystal in the background is simultaneously forming and we can feel the energy of the lotus flower there.

A photograph of dolphins
「イルカ」の写真

イルカはそのヒーリング能力などについてもよく知られています。ノーブルさ、つまり「気高さ」とか「高貴さ」においては、もっとも高い評価のできる結晶になりました。
「はは～ん。なるほどな。あなたがたはやっぱりすごい！」という感じです。

Dolphins are well known for their healing power also. In terms of nobility or nobleness, this became the most highly acclaimed crystal. It seems to say, "See, it really is true. You are amazing, all of you!"

Water that was shown a photograph of Mt. Fuji

「富士山」の写真

美しい富士山の写真を撮ることで有名な、ロッキー田中さんが撮影した写真の上に水を置きました。
神々しい日輪の色合いが、結晶の左上部に反映されています。
（こうごう）

We placed the water on top of a photograph taken by Mr. Rocky Tanaka.
He is famous for taking photographs of beautiful Mt. Fuji.
The hues of a sublime solar orb are reflected at the top left of the crystal.

Water which was shown the characters for "Sun" (right)

「太陽」という文字（右）

太陽については、写真を見せたもの、文字を見せたもの、同じ様な波動を感じます。現実の姿と言霊の世界が一致しているようでもあります。言ってみれば表裏一体、虚実の一致、偽りのない姿……。
考え過ぎかもしれませんが、そう思います。

Concerning the sun, the sense here is of water picking up the same HADO, whether it is from being shown writing or a photograph. I think the actual form and the world of "Kototama" are the same. In other words the front and the back are one, emptiness and fullness are uniform. The form has no deception in it. Perhaps that is stretching it , but I believe so.

Sun

Water which was shown a photograph of the sun (left)

「太陽」の写真（左）

「太陽の本」伊藤 凡恵　著
"The Sun's Book" by Namie Ito

Water which was shown the characters for "Earth" (right)

「地球」という文字（右）

NASAから打ち上げられた人工衛星からとった実際の地球と、文字の波動は少し異なり、写真の方は少し小さくなっている気がします。
文字の方が躍動感があり、それに比べて写真を見せた方はこぢんまりとまとまって……。
がんばれ地球！

The shot taken from NASA's artificial satellite of the actual Earth, and the one taken of the vibration of the characters are a little different. It feels like the one from the photograph is a little smaller. The crystal based on writing has a more lively feel, and compared to it, that of the crystal shown the photograph is more compacted together.
Hold out, Earth!

Earth

Water that was shown a photograph of Earth (left)

「地球」の写真（左）

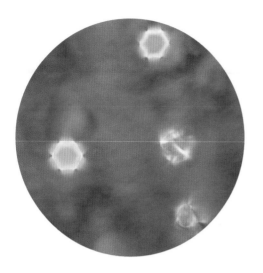

ほたるの里の湧き水／Spring water from the home of fireflies

ほたるの里と呼ばれているのは、新潟県のある町。この里に温泉が出るということで、ボーリングを続けた人がいましたが、温泉ではなくて、きれいな湧き水がでてきたとか。たぶんホタルは、温泉よりきれいな水のほうをご所望だったのではないでしょうか。ホタルのように光り輝く結晶です。

The place that is called the 'home of fireflies' is located in a town in Niigata prefecture. It was said there is a hotspring source in this village, so someone kept on drilling in search of it. Apparently it was not a hot spring but clean fresh spring water that came out. Could it not be that the fireflies had a desire for fresh water rather than a
thermal spring? This is a crystal that sparkles like the light of fireflies.

「ＥＭ」という文字を見せた水

Water that was shown the letters for "EM"

「ＥＭ」という文字を見せたらできた結晶です。真ん中に「ＥＭ」の生みの親である、いつも笑顔の比嘉照男先生のニコニコ顔が見えるようです。

「ＥＭ」とは……有用微生物群（Effective Microorganisms）のこと。
土壌の改良、畜産、水産、ゴミや下水処理に応用するもの

This is the crystal formed on being shown the letters "EM". In the centre it seems we can see the ever smiling face of Mr. Teruo Higa, the man who gave birth to the "EM" phenomenon.

"EM" is the abbreviation for "Effective Microorganisms" and is applicable for soil improvement, the livestock industry, fisheries and garbage/sewage disposal treatment etc.

EM

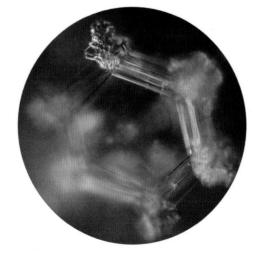

「ありがとう」と「ばかやろう」の文字を同時に見せた水

Water that was simultaneously shown the words, "Thank you" and "You fool"

予測はもっと混乱した結晶になるかと思っていました。ところが、「ありがとう」は「ばかやろう」の力を消して、透明な六角形の結晶を見せてくれました。「ありがとう」の波動の力強さをあらためて感じます。

I was expecting a much less beautiful crystal being formed. "Thank you" cancelled the power of "You fool" and showed us a transparent hexagonal crystal. Once again you feel the strength of thank you's vibration.

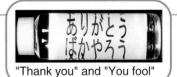

"Thank you" and "You fool"

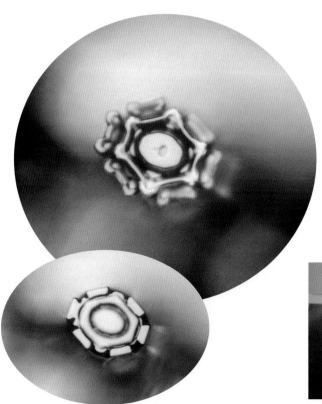

ミステリーサークルの写真を見せた水
Water which was shown a photograph of a crop circle

イギリス南部にしばしば現れるというミステリーサークル。
「ジャパニーズ折り紙」という名前のついたミステリーサーク
ルの写真の上に水を置いて、聞いてみました。
やはり、UFOとしか思えないような結晶ができましたが、さ
て……。

Crop circles, as they are called, often appear in Southern
England. We placed the water on top of a photograph of a
crop circle known as 'Japanese origami' to see what would
come up. And look, a crystal formed that looks like it could
be nothing other than a UFO. Well...

写真に写った雪の結晶たち
The crystals of the snowflake photographs

スイスのホテルの前で、同時刻に撮った写真です。
雪の形が違っています。私が写っている方は六角形。
妻（和子）が写っている方は、まん丸となっています。
ということは、妻のおかげで私は六角形の結晶が撮れて
いるようです。妻に感謝!!
（妻が撮った方の写真の雪が六角形だから）

These photographs were taken at the same time in
front of a hotel in Switzerland. The snowflake
pattern is different in these two photographs. The
photograph I am in has hexagonal shapes.
The photograph my wife, Kazuko is in, has circular
shapes. Thanks to my wife, it seems that hexagonal
crystals have been taken in mine. I do appreciate
my wife!
(I do appreciate my wife because the snowflakes
that she took a photograph of are hexagonal)

第7章

不思議の世界

　知恵、宇宙、愛・感謝という文字を、日本語、英語、ドイツ語などそれぞれに、水に見せてみました。元の水は、同じ基準の精製水を使用しました。

　その結果得られた結晶は、文字が違ったにもかかわらず、各国語とも非常に類似性のある形を示してくれました。私の持論は『言葉は大自然の振動によってつくられている』ということ。国によって自然も違い、言葉も違いますから、その振動も違ってきます。しかし、大自然の摂理そのものは変わりませんから、同じ意味をもつ言葉は、同じような形を示したのではないでしょうか。

波動とは言葉なり

言葉とは大自然の産物なり

ゆえに美しき言葉は美しき自然をつくり

悪しき言葉は悪しき自然を成す

これ宇宙の根元なり

Chapter 7　The world of wonder
We showed water the words "Wisdom", "Cosmos",and "Love · Thanks" in each of these languages: Japanese, English and German.
The original water we used was the same standard refined water.

The crystals we got as a result, in spite of the differences in the words, showed us shapes with great similarity for each language. I am of the opinion that, "Words are created by mother nature's vibration". Therefore, when languages differ depending on the country, the vibration differs as well. However, the providence of nature itself does not change, so the words which have the same meaning probably show similar forms.

HADO creates words
Words are the vibrations of nature
Therefore beautiful words create beautiful nature
Ugly words create ugly nature
This is the root of the Universe

いずれもよく似ています。真ん中の部分が黒く抜けているのも、同じです。

智慧には悪智慧や浅智慧もありますから、中身が大切ということなのでしょうか。

They all look quite similar. The dark void in the centre part is the same.

In wisdom, since there is serpentine wisdom and shallow wisdom, could it mean that its content is important?

"Wisdom" in Japanese

日本語　智慧

英語 **Wisdom**

Wisdom

ドイツ語 **Weisheit**

Wisdom

いずれも撮影日時も撮影者も違います。
でも、同じような形になりました。

All of these shots were taken by different people on different dates
and times. However, they all ended up with similar forms.

Cosmos

"Cosmos" in Japanese

日本語　宇宙

英語 **Cosmos**

Cosmos

ギリシャ語 **Kosmos**

Cosmos

「愛・感謝」は結晶写真の女王様です。
大自然の摂理は、この2種類の言葉によって成り立っていると、私が主張するゆえんです。

"Love・Thanks" is the queen of all crystal photographs.
This is the reason I emphasize that the providence of nature consists of these two words.

Love・Thanks

"Love ・Thanks" in English
英語 **Love ・ Thanks**

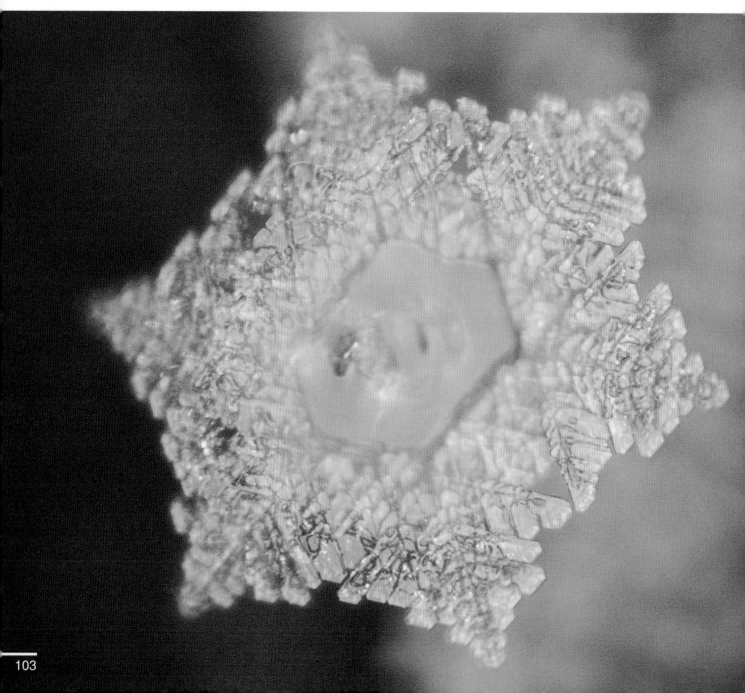

"Love ・Thanks" in Japanese
日本語　愛・感謝

Love・Thanks

"Love ・Thanks" in German
ドイツ語
Liebe・Danken

Love・　Thanks

ごらんのように全部ポジティブで良い結晶ができました。

世界中の言語の「ありがとう」を結晶にして、国連総会で発表できたらいいなと思います。いろいろな言語の「ありがとう」を巻末の住所かメールアドレスまで送っていただければ幸いです。

As you can see, all the crystals were positive and fine.

I would love to present crystals of the word "Thank you" in world languages, at the United Nations General Assembly. Therefore, I would be happy if you could send a variety of "Thank you" in many languages to the address or E-mail address written at the end of this book.

"Thank you" in Italian
イタリア語　Grazie

Thank you

"Thank you" in French
フランス語　Merci

Thank you

"Thank you" in Chinese

中国語 多謝

Thank you

"Thank you" in Tagalog

タガログ語
Maraming Salamat

Thank you

"Thank you" in Malaysian

マレーシア語
Terima Kasih

Thank you

Wisdom and compassion
智慧と慈悲

2つの言葉を合わせると、2タイプの結晶ができました。

1つは、智慧がしっかりと反映されたもの（99ページ）。2つめは、包みこむような慈愛の言霊が反映したもの。2つの言葉がそれぞれに、その姿を見せてくれているようです。

When two words were combined two types of crystals were created.

In the first one wisdom is clearly reflected (page 99). In the second one, the Kototama of an embracing benevolence is reflected. Each of these two words seems to show that aspect.

Wisdom and compassion

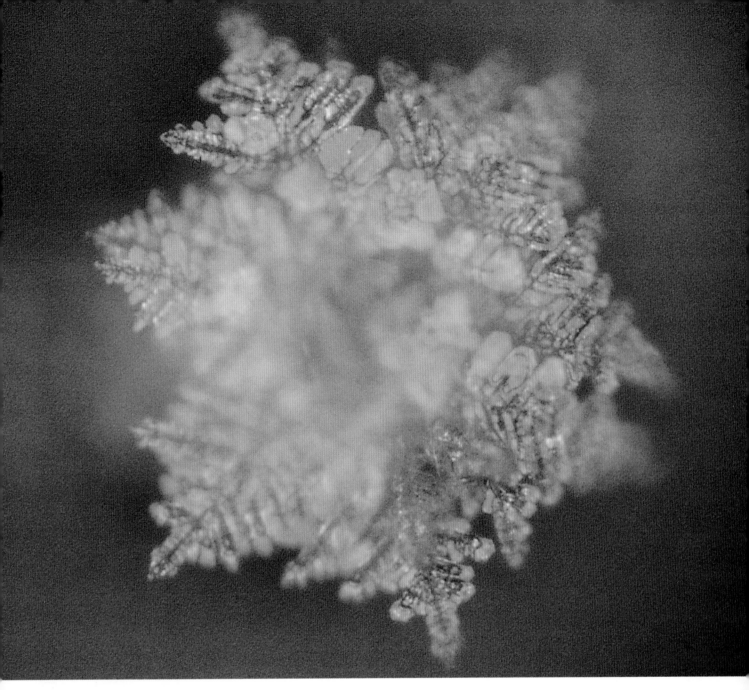

Spirit

霊

いったい何角形でしょうか。予想通り、これは三次元の世界のものではなく、それ以上の次元の情報をもって……しかもぼやけている結晶が撮れました。

How many angles does this have ?
As expected, it doesn't look like one from the third dimension but one with information of more dimensions than that. On top of that, we got a blurred crystal.

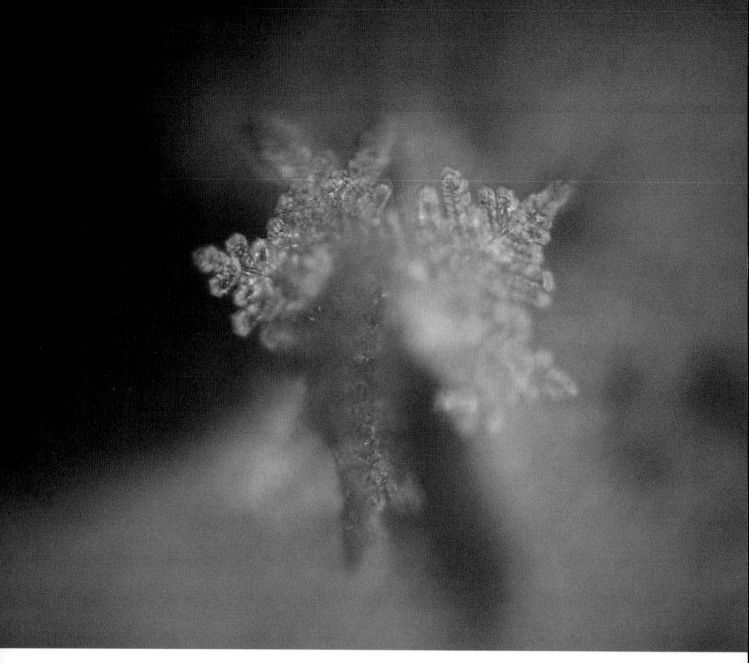

War

戦争

大自然の中の生存競争と、戦争とはまったく違います。
もちろん、ごらんのように壊滅的な結晶となりました。
戦争は、何も創造しないということなのです。

The struggle for existence in nature and war are completely different. Of course, as you can see, the crystal ended up annihilated. War creates nothing.

War

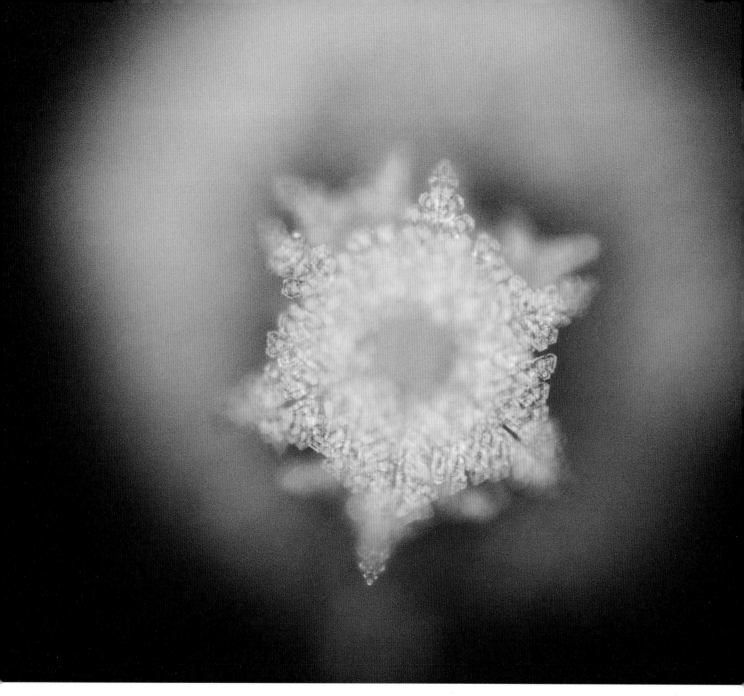

Peace

Peace
平和

平和という文字を見た水の結晶は、星のように美しくなりました。もうひとつの結晶が重なり合っていますが、他を邪魔していませんね。まさに和しています。

The crystal of the water which saw the word "Peace" became as beautiful as a star. Then another crystal overlaps, yet it doesn't disturb the other. It really shows peace.

意識と場

1年ほど前に企画したあるシンポジウムのテーマを水に見せました。「美しいけれども、芯の部分のアキが大きすぎる……どういうことだろう」と、思っていたら、果たしてこのシンポジウムは、あまり人が集まりませんでした。

We showed water to the theme of a symposium which was organized about a year ago. "It is beautiful but the void at the core part is too big.....what could this be?" I was wondering about that, and just as I thought, not many people had gathered at this symposium.

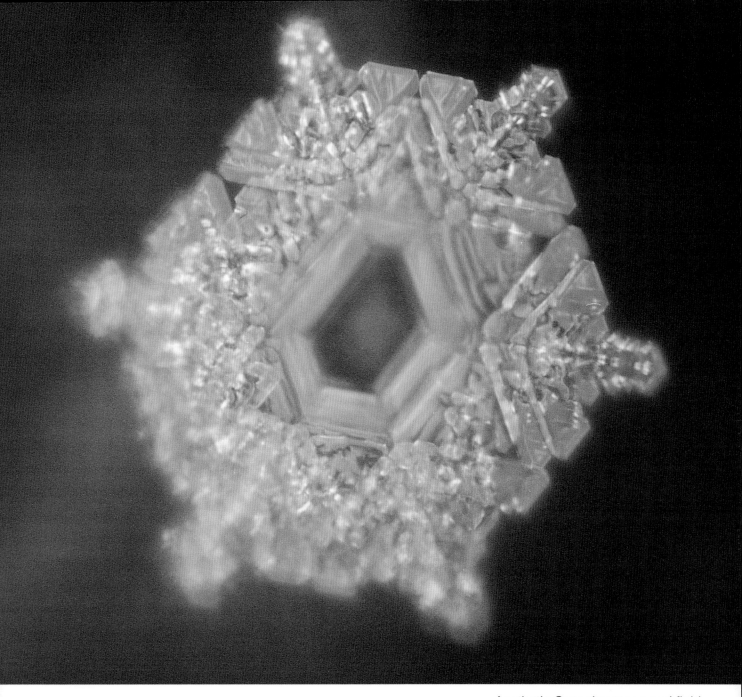

美意識と場

Aesthetic Consciousness and field

意識と場に「美」を一文字、加えたところ、見事に美しく結晶してくれました。
あいまいな表現ではなく、本当の目的を示す内容を素直にはっきりと伝え、話し、書くことが大切なのではと思います。

Just one word, "Aesthetic" was added to consciousness and field and a splendidly aesthetic crystal appeared. It seems to be important to convey, speak or write the details indicating the true purpose rather than expressing it vaguely.

Fire

火

火はやはり、燃え上がるエネルギーを感じさせる
結晶ですね。

Fire does indeed feel like upward burning energy in
the crystal.

Fire

Water

水

包容力のある、ゆったりとした感じの結晶にな
りました。

It became a crystal with a magnanimous and relaxed
feeling.

Water

サンスクリット語 (梵語) ・インドの古語　祈りの言葉

ॐ नमः शिवाय
शिवाय नम ॐ

「オーム」シヴァ神を礼拝します
The word OM praising the Hindu
God "Shiva"

シバ神をたたえる言葉を見せた水を、ヨーロッパの知人に頼まれて撮影しました。
なんともすばらしい結晶になりました。「バリ島のケチャ（73ページ）」ともよく似ています。
曼陀羅のようにも見えるし、女性たちが集まってつくるキルトのようでもあります。

I was asked to take a photograph of the Hindu God "Shiva" by an acquaintance in Europe, and so did.
It became such a wonderful crystal! It also looks similar to the crystal called "Kecak from Bali (page 73)"
It looks like a Mandala as well, or can be seen as the pattern on quilts which women gather together to
make.

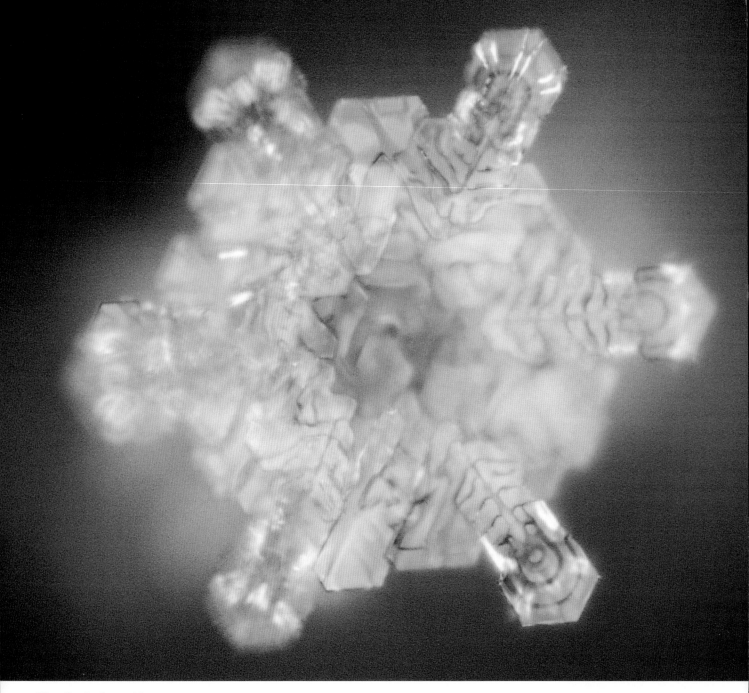

The God of wealth

福の神

日本で古くから親しまれている神様です。
大きく、クリエイティブで、成長の勢いがあり、広がっていくような形をしています。

This has been a favoured God since ancient times in Japan.
It has a huge, creative, vigorous feeling of growth and also an expansive form.

The God of wealth

The God of poverty

The God of poverty

貧乏神

結晶ができないのではないかと心配しましたが、がんばってきれいな形をつくってくれました。
ときには貧乏神が来ても、いいことがあるのかもしれません。
それにしても日本人はなんでも神様にしてしまいます。やはり八百万（やおよろず）の神の国ですね。

We were worried that maybe the crystal would not appear but it made an effort to form a beautiful pattern.
It is probably a good thing to have the god of poverty show up sometime. Somehow, Japanese have a
tendency to interpret everything as Gods. Japan is after all, a land of myriads of Gods and deities.

第8章

水に気持ちを伝えたら

　もうすでに何年も、私たちは水に対して、いろいろなことを試みています。

そして、水はそのつど、誠心誠意その答えを見せてくれます。

　ここでは、これまでの研究と実験の中から、水にみんなで祈ったり、水に感謝の言葉をかけて、

人の気持ちを伝えてみたらどうなるか試してみたものをご紹介させていただきます。

chapter 8　Conveying our feelings to water
We are testing a variety of things with water, and water shows a response wholeheartedly on each occasion that we do this.
In this section, we'd like to introduce what we can from our research and experiments on water that everyone prayed to, and
water that had been given words of gratitude.

藤原ダム／Fujiwara Dam

祈祷前／Before the prayer　　祈祷後／After the prayer

藤原ダムの祈祷から琵琶湖の浄化へ

　最近は琵琶湖が年々汚れてきていると言われています。琵琶湖は人々のふるさと。マザーレイク、日本の子宮的存在です。子宮の中にある羊水が汚れては心配です。

　『水からの伝言・1』に私は、1997年10月に群馬県の藤原ダムで行った加持祈祷による水の浄化を紹介いたしました。その実験の結果に深く感銘し、同じことを琵琶湖で行いたいと考えました。

　1999年7月25日、朝4時30分、350名の人が集まり、琵琶湖に向かって言葉をささげました。

　当時97歳だった『大断言』の塩谷信男先生も、ごいっしょに祈ってくださいました。この結果、私たちは世間があっと驚くような、すごい成果を得ることになったのです。

その成果とは……？

　その日から1カ月と2日たった8月27日、地元の有力新聞社である京都新聞社がびっくりし、とても喜びました。

今年は琵琶湖の水に対する苦情が減った、水藻の分布状態もよくなり、水の悪臭がなくなったというのです。

　2000年の9月25日にサンマーク出版より発刊された「自在力2」でその著者、塩谷信男先生は次のように述べられています。

琵琶湖の水へ祈願の念をおくる ▶
Sending thoughts of the prayer to
Lake Biwa

◀ 琵琶湖に向かって「ありがとう」の気持ちを伝える
Facing Lake Biwa and sending out feelings of thanks

From the prayer at Fujiwara Dam to the purification of Lake Biwa

They say that year by year the water of Lake Biwa is getting dirtier. Lake Biwa is the people's home. It is the mother lake, the equivalent of Japan's womb. It's a cause for concern if the amniotic fluid of the womb is dirty.

In the "Message from Water 1", I introduced the purification of water by the incantation of a prayer at the Fujiwara dam in Gunma prefecture in October of 1997. I was deeply impressed by the result of that experiment and decided on doing the same thing at Lake Biwa.

On the 25th of July 1999 at 04:30 in the morning, 350 people gathered and offered their words facing Lake Biwa.
Praying with us at that time was the then 97 year old creator of the "Grand Declaration", Mr. Nobuo Shioya. The result of that was an incredible success that truly surprised us, the public at large.

One month and two days from that time on August 27th the influential local newspaper company, Kyoto Shinbun, was both surprised and delighted. "This year the complaints about Lake Biwa's water have decreased, the condition of aquatic algae distribution has improved and the foul odour of the water has disappeared."

Concerning the outcome of that, here is how Mr. Shioya described it in his book 'Jizairyoku 2' (Self sustaining power 2) published by Sunmark Press on September 25, 2000:

1999年8月27日の京都新聞
The Kyoto Shinbun newspaper
1999, August 27th

わが国最大の湖で、関西地方の水瓶でもある滋賀県の琵琶湖も例にもれず、汚染がひどく、水は汚れて悪臭を放ち、かつての美しい湖岸やヨシの群落などはもうほとんど見られなくなったといいます。かわりに毎年夏になると、コカナダモという外来の水草が異常繁殖して湖面を覆い、これが腐って近辺に悪臭をまき散らすので、県が大がかりな刈り取り作業を行うことが、もう二十年以上も続いているといいます。

ところが昨年（平成十一年）の夏だけは、どういうわけかこの水草がほとんど発生せず、例年なら役所に殺到する悪臭への苦情も、まったく寄せられなかった。その原因の見当がつかないので、関係者はみんな首をひねっていると新聞に報じられていました。

いわば突然、「有が無になる」現象が琵琶湖の水面に起こったわけですが、この"奇跡"も、わたしは思いの力で説明できると考えています。というのも、それを起こした張本人のひとりが、ほかならぬこのわたしだからです。

この年、波動の研究をしている人たちが中心になって、琵琶湖の水をきれいにしようという催し事が開かれました。琵琶湖の水がきれいになれば、日本中の水が浄化されるという古くからの言い伝えがあり、波動や言霊の力でそれを実践しようという集まりです。そこにわたしも呼ばれて、湖畔のホテルまで出向き、正心調息法に関する講演を行いました。

そして翌日の未明、琵琶湖の湖岸に三百余人の参加者が集合し、わたしをまん中にして湖面に向かうと、昇りくる朝日を正面から浴びながら、「大断言」を唱えたのです。

「宇宙の無限の力が凝り凝って、
真の大和のみ世が生り成った」

とわたしが先導するかたちで、全員がこの大断言の言葉を十回唱和しました。

大断言とは文字どおり、宇宙に満ちる無限のエネルギーを活用することによって、世界平和を実現する力強い言葉。それを既成のこととして強くいいきる断言の言葉です。

これを発することで、宇宙無限力が吹きこまれた言霊のパワーが周囲の事物に広がり、浸透して、世界の平和をはじめ多くの願望達成や幸福が人びとにもたらされる。そのもっとも力強い想念の言葉であり、また、もっとも強力に想念の実現を後押しする言葉のことです。

その唱和がすむと、すぐにその場を失礼して、老齢のわたしはホテルへ帰りました。それが昨年の七月のこと。そして、「琵琶湖で毎夏、湖面を覆うほど異常繁茂する外来藻『コカナダモ』が、今年は、ほとんど湖面に姿を現さない。例年、悪臭に対して滋賀県などに寄せられる苦情も今年はまったくなく、県による刈り取り量もごくわずかだ」（京都新聞平成十一年八月二十七日付）と新聞報道されたのは、それから一か月後の八月末のことでした。

しかし、それは不思議現象でもなければ原因のないことでもない。大断言に込めて発したわたしたちの想念が悪臭のもとである水草の発生を抑え、湖水をきれいに変えたのです。万物の調和と安定を願うわたしたちの思い、それが大断言によって草や水にはっきり伝わり、その性質を変え、自然の汚れを浄化してしまった ― 多くの人は気づかないが、そこには明瞭な因果関係が存在しているのです。

このように人の心だけではなく、この世界に存在するすべての生命あるもの、あるいは水のような自然界の物質もふくめた万物万象は、わたしたち人間の思いに感応するものです。その想念を受け入れて、状態や性質を変えて行くものなのです。

塩谷信男著「自在力2」より

The largest lake in our land, the "water jar" for the whole Kansai district, Lake Biwa in Shiga prefecture is an example without exception of horrendous pollution, with foul smelling and dirty water. No longer can we see the beautiful lake shore or the stock of ditch reeds there. Instead, every summer the surface of the lake is covered with a foreign species of aquatic plant called 'kokanada' algae which then putrefies. It spreads a foul odour around the area, and so for over twenty years the prefecture has been carrying out a large scale operation to weed it out. However, last year (1999) during that summer only, for some reason this aquatic plant hardly emerged at all, and there were no complaints made to the city office as it is usually swamped with during a normal year.
It was reported in the newspapers that none of the parties concerned could ascertain the cause of this and that they were all shaking their heads over it.

Naturally that would be the case when 'something that was there is no more', as in the phenomenon which occurred on the surface of Lake Biwa. This "miracle" also can be explained I think through the power of thought. It's a fact that, as one of the ringleaders of this happening, nobody else but me could know that. In that year an event was held to clean up the waters of Lake Biwa by a group mainly involved in researching HADO. If the waters of Biwa were to become clean, an old saying had it that all of Japan's water would be purified, and so this congregation of people was there to use the power of HADO and Kotodama to try to do just that.
I was also invited there and so headed for a hotel by the lake side where I gave a lecture on the method of "right mind and breath control". Then on the next morning sometime, about three hundred participants assembled on the lake shore. With myself in the middle, we faced the lake's surface and as the rising sun came up before us we chanted "The Grand Declaration".
"The eternal power of the universe has gathered itself to create a world with true and grand harmony."
I led the group in doing this and everyone performed the intoning of the words ten times. "The Grand Declaration" as it literally says, by utilizing the limitless energy filling the universe, is a powerful statement to actualize world peace. These are words that can be clearly stated strongly as an established fact. By vocalising this, the power of Kotodama, infused with the eternal energy of the universe, spreads to surrounding things and penetrates them, giving people world peace to begin with, many wishes fulfilled and happiness. That most powerful notion in words is also a statement that boosts that notion into actualisation most strongly.

After cheering in chorus, I quickly excused myself and, being an old man, returned to the hotel. That happened last year in July. And then came this: "Every summer on Lake Biwa the foreign species of algae called kokanada, which almost covers the lake as it flourishes abnormally, is practically out of sight this year. In a normal year the complaints of foul odour which come in to Shiga prefecture, have been nil this year and the amount of algae cleaned up by the prefecture is a mere pittance." It was a month later at the end of August when this was reported in the press (The Kyoto Shinbun newspaper 1999, August 27th)

However, if that was not a mysterious phenomenon it is still not something without a cause. Our thoughts that were sent out imbued with "The Grand Declaration" curbed the emergence of an aquatic plant which was the source of a foul odour, and transformed the surface of the lake into a clean state. Our thoughts, requesting harmony and stability for all things through "The Grand Declaration" were transmitted clearly to grass and water, changing their qualities and purifying nature's pollution—although many people do not realize it, there you have a clear causal relationship existing.

In this fashion, it is not only human minds but also all life forms in this world containing all things and phenomena, including substances in nature like water which respond to our human thoughts. They accept those thoughts and it changes their condition and quality.

From 'Jizairyoku 2' by Nobuo Shioya

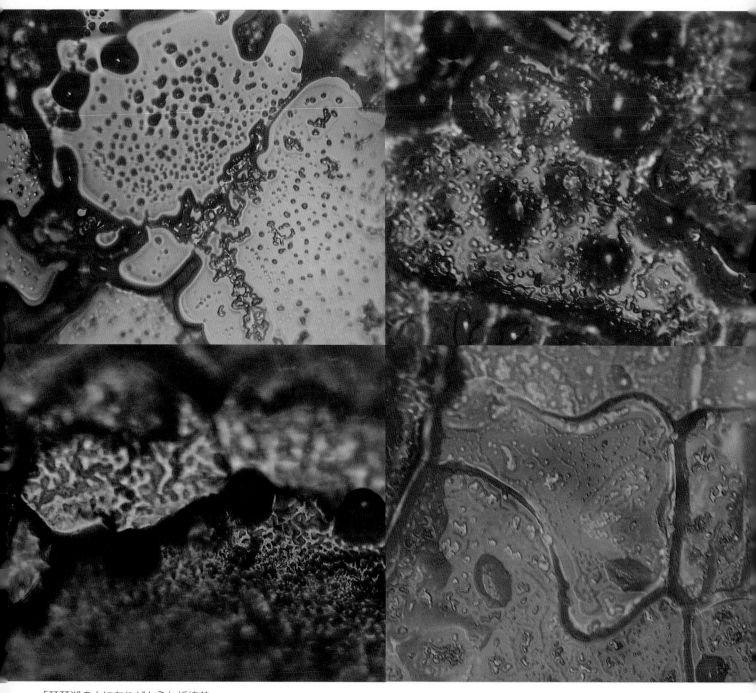

「琵琶湖の水にありがとう」祈祷前
"Thank you to the water of Lake Biwa" Before the prayer

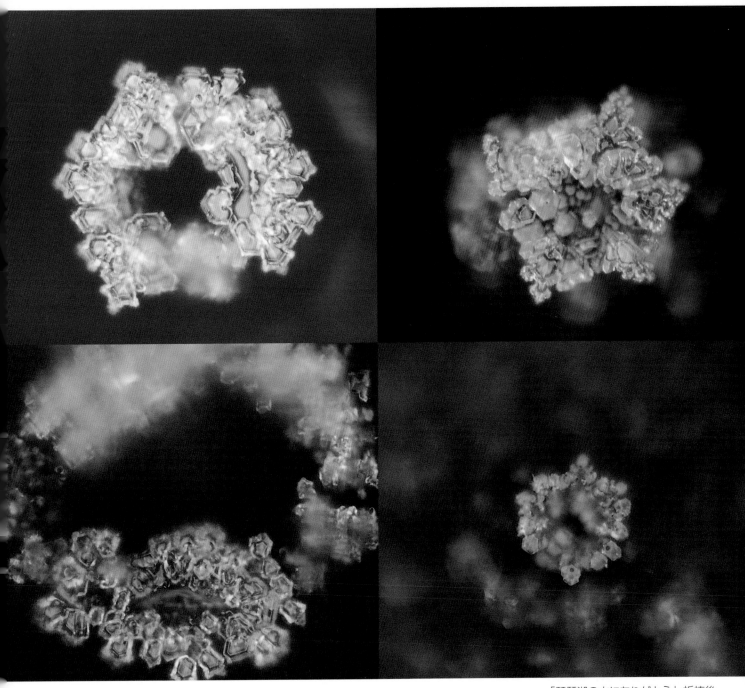

琵琶湖祈願の半年後／Half a year after the Lake Biwa prayer

水中のダイオキシン
超音波を流し分解
湖沼の浄化に活用
大阪府立大教授開発

水に含まれているダイオキシンやPCB（ポリ塩化ビフェニール）などの有機塩素化合物系の有害物質を、超音波を利用しほぼ完全に分解する技術が大阪府立大工学部の前田泰昭教授（環境化学）によって開発されたことが十五日、明らかになった。周波数二百㎑の超音波を水中に流し、ごく微細な〔気泡〕を水中に生成させると、気泡が化合物を吸着する上、破裂する際に化合物を分解できるという。汚染された湖沼の水質浄化に活用でき、大気のオゾン層を破壊するフロンも分解できそうだ。これらの物質は分解しにくい性質を持つため処理法の確立が課題とされており、技術が実用化されれば国内外に大きな反響を呼びそうだ。

超音波は人間が聞こえる位の気泡が発生する。破裂「からの水圧に負けて破裂す音域（十㎑～二万㎑）より気泡は瞬間的に五千もまず○・一マイクロ秒（一る際、気泡は瞬間的に五千も高い音。水中で加圧と減千万分の一秒）程度と短命度を超える熱と約千気圧の波により、ミクロン単だが、加圧の波による周の圧力を発しているという。

最近の研究で分かってきた。着する。気泡が破裂する位の気泡が発生する。熱と高圧で、無害化される有機塩素化合物は水の気泡とガスと塩化物イオンに相性が悪く、この気泡に吸される」という仕組み。

2000年4月16日の産経新聞
The Sankei Newspaper
—April 16th. 2000,

「ありがとう琵琶湖」のキャンペーンのあと、大阪府立大学の前田教授の発表された記事（産経新聞）にも驚きました。この記事から、私たちが唱えた言葉のオーバートーンとして、超音波が宇宙エリアのエネルギーと共鳴して、効果が出たのではないかと考えられるのです。

私たちは「ありがとう琵琶湖」キャンペーンのあとも、ずっと定期的に結晶の撮影を続けました。2000年の1月までの半年足らず、琵琶湖の水の結晶はきれいでした。

ところが2000年8月には、また悪臭がもどってしまいました。

琵琶湖の大きさに対して350人というのは、ちょっと人数が足りなかったようです。もともと、30万人の人に集まって手をつないでもらい、琵琶湖を取り囲んで祈ろう……という計画でしたが、準備不足でした。

もし時間がたっぷりあれば、きっともっと長い間、琵琶湖の水の結晶を美しく保つことができたであろうと確信しています。

After the "Thank you, Lake Biwa" campaign, we were also surprised by an article (Sankei newspaper) which was published by Professor Maeda of Osaka Prefectural University. From this article, it is possible to consider that the effect resulted from ultrasonic waves resonating with the cosmic energy, as an overtone of the words we intoned.

We have continued to take photos of the crystals regularly since the "Thank you, Lake Biwa" campaign. The crystals of Lake Biwa's water turned out beautifully in only less than six months up to January 2000. However, in August 2000, the bad odour returned again. Given the size of Lake Biwa, only three hundred and fifty people were not enough. The original plan was to gather three hundred thousand people and all stand hand in hand around the lake to pray.... but we were not prepared enough.
If there had been sufficient time, I am sure that we could have kept the beautiful crystal of Lake Biwa water much longer.

祈りの後／After the prayer

祈りの前／Before the prayer

At the Zurich seminar in Switzerland

スイス チューリッヒ セミナーにて

世界各国のセミナーで、琵琶湖の話をします。そしてその場でセミナー参加者が手をつないで、お水がきれいになりますように……という儀式を行っています。それぞれのお国の言葉で、琵琶湖と同じように大断言を訳し、それぞれの祈りをささげます。そして意識と、言葉と祈り、ローソクなどの小さな火とがいっしょになったとき、その集合意識は確実に水に伝わることが分かってきました。チューリッヒ湖の水の結晶もとてもきれいになりました。

I talk about Lake Biwa at my seminars all over the world. The seminar participants in each area hold hands with each other that the water may become clean.....it is a ceremony like that. Each individual prays using "The Grand Declaration" as we did at Lake Biwa, translated into each individual's language. It became clear that when conciousness, words, prayer and a little fire join together, that collective conciousness is most surely transmitted into water. The crystal of Zurich Lake water also became very beautiful.

祈りの前／Before the prayer

126

▲ 祈りの後／After the prayer

At a ceremony in Lucerne, Switzerland

スイス ルツェルン セレモニーにて

▲ 祈りの前／Before the prayer

▲ 祈りの後／After the prayer

スイス コンスタンス セミナーにて

コンスタンス湖畔における祈りの結果です。

The result of the prayer at the lakeshore, Lake Constance.

▲ 祈りの前／Before the prayer

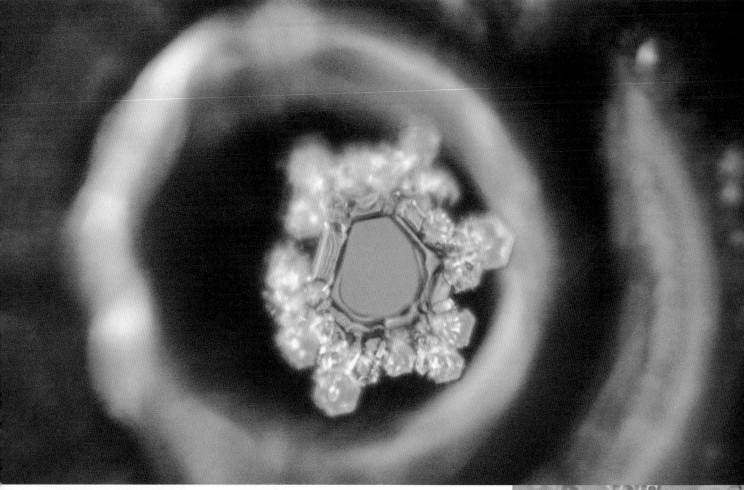

▲ 祈りの後／After the prayer

At the seminar in the Bahamas
バハマ セミナーにて

バハマでも、14〜15人で水に声をかけました。その結果、結晶はとてもきれいになりました。

参加者が手をつなぐと、それは「結界（修行などのために一定の場所を特定すること）」をつくり、その効果が長持ちすることも分かってきました。

それにつけても、1999年の夏の琵琶湖で、30万人が手をつなぎ、琵琶湖を取り囲んで祈っていたら……と本当に残念です。

Also in the Bahamas, 14 to15 people talked to the water. As a result, the water became very clean.

When the participants held each other's hands, it was discovered that the circle creates a 'Kekkai' (A Buddhist term meaning to make a protective boundary for a particular area) and within it the effects are maintained longer. That reminds me of the summer of 1999 at lake Biwa, where if three hundred thousand people hand in hand had surrounded the lake and prayed....it is truly a pity.

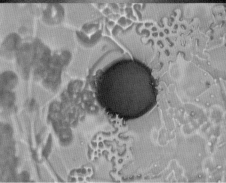

▲ 祈りの前／Before the prayer

▲ 祈りの後／After the prayer

At the Lake Eucha purification festival in Tulsa City, Oklahoma State

オクラホマ州タルサ市
ウチイ湖浄化フェスティバルにて

オクラホマ・タルサ在住の石田俊明さんが中心になって、30人ほど集まったフェスティバルでも、水にお祈りをささげました。

Mr.Toshiaki Ishida, a resident of Tulsa, Oklahoma leads the prayer for water at a festival where about 30 people gathered to pray for water.

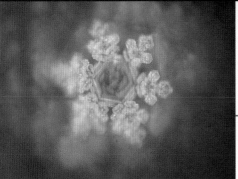

▲ 祈りの最中／During the prayer

▲ 祈りの前／Before the prayer

子どもたちからの手紙に感謝！

　『水からの伝言・1』を出版して、最初にその内容を認めてくださったのは、お母さんたちであり、学校の先生方でした。彼らはただ単に、結晶を見るだけでなく、実際に子どもたちといっしょに楽しみ、さまざまな実験をしてくださいました。

この本をつくるにあたって、私が最大の目的とした「生活の場で使ってほしい」ということを実践してくださったのは彼らでした。

　子どもたちはあたかも純粋な水の結晶のように反応してくれています。

この子どもたちを取りまく人々は、これからもどんどん光輝く結晶をつくり続ける人生を歩んでくれると信じています。

Thank you for the letters from children

The initial recognition of the content we received on publishing "The Message from Water 1" came from mothers and school teachers. They didn't simply just look at the crystals but actually had fun with the children taking part in the experiments. My greatest aim in the creation of that book, to have it used in daily life situations, was actually carried out by them. Children react very much like the crystals of pure water.

I believe it is these children who from now on will live their lives like the ongoing creation of crystals, sparkling with ever-growing light.

『ありがとう』『ばかやろう』の水で
ヒマワリを育てました

江本勝さんへ

こんにちは、とつぜんのお手紙でごめんなさい。今年の春に、ある雑誌で江本さんの記事を見ました。「ありがとう」と「ばかやろう」の文字を水に見せたときの結晶に、びっくりしました。信じられない気持ちでいっぱいでした。

それで私は、夏休みの研究にこの水でヒマワリを育ててみようと思いました。

決めたことは、

◆ 同じ決まりでいっしょに育てること

◆ 文字だけでなく自分で声かけもすること

◆ 水は朝と夜、200ccずつ、ひまわりにあげる

1、6月 2日、タネを入れた封筒と植木鉢と水をやるペットボトルに、それぞれ「ありがとう」と「ばかやろう」と書きました。

2、6月 6日、タネをまきました。ねんのために2鉢ずつ育てました。

3、6月20日、「ありがとう」は2鉢、「ばかやろう」は1鉢、芽が出ました。

　　　　「ありがとう」の鉢はクキも葉もツルツルとして丸い。

　　　　「ばかやろう」の鉢は、ぎざぎざで赤っぽかった。

　　　　ほんとうなのかなあ。偶然なのかなあ。

I grew sunflowers with "Thank you" and "You fool" water

To Mr. Masaru Emoto,

From Mai Adachi (Ten years old, Gifu city)

Hello, excuse me for writing to you all of a sudden, Mr. Emoto. I found your article in a magazine this spring. I was surprised at the crystals that the letters "Thank you" and "You fool" were shown to. It was unbelievable.

Then I decided to grow sunflowers with that water for the summer holiday project.

Things I decided to do:

◆ Growing them under the same conditions.

◆ Not only by letters but also by speaking to the plants myself.

◆ Watering the sunflowers with 200cc of water every morning and evening.

1. June　2nd.　On the envelope containing the seeds, the planting pots and the plastic bottles which I used for watering everyday, I wrote "Thank you" and "You fool" on each one of them.

2. June　6th.　I planted the seeds. Just in case, I had decided to grow two pots each.

3. June 20th.　Two of the "Thank you" and one of the "You fool" pots sprouted.

　　　　The stems and leaves of the "Thank you" pots were smooth and roundish.

　　　　The "You fool" pot was spiky and had a reddish colour.

　　　　Is this for real?　Or a coincidence?

132

「ありがとう」のひまわり
"Thank you" sunflower

「ばかやろう」のひまわり
"You fool" sunflower

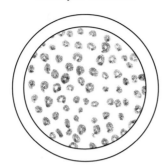
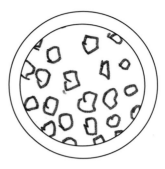

下から50cmのところを切断して、茎の断面を顕微鏡で調べた。

Looking through a microscope at the cross section of the stems that
hadbeen cut 50 centimetres from the bottom

イラスト・足立麻衣さん／Illustrated by Mai Adachi

4、6月22日　「ばかやろう」の芽も出てきた「うれしいなぁ」。

5、6月25日　「ありがとう」はまるまるしてきた。

　　　　　　「ばかやろう」の葉はぎざぎざ。

6、6月28日　「ありがとう」は背が高い。

　　　　　　「ばかやろう」は本葉がまがったり、穴があいてしまっている。心配。

　　　　　　これからもみんな元気に育ってほしいけど、差もついてほしいです。

7、7月2日　「ありがとう」はクキに毛がはえて、私の背の高さをこえそう。

　　　　　　「ばかやろう」は本葉がしわくちゃ。でも、差がでないような気がするな。

8、クキの断面を顕微鏡で見る。（上のイラスト）

4. June 22nd. The "You fool" pot's sprout came out. "I'm so happy!"
5. June 25th. "Thank you" started to get roundish.
　　　　　　　 "You fool" leaves were spiky.
6. June 28th. "Thank you" were tall.
　　　　　　　 "You fool" The leaves are bent and had holes. I'm worried!
　　　　　　　 I want all of them to grow healthy but on the other hand, I want them to be different.
7. July 2nd.　 "Thank you" started to have fur on the stems and looked like it would get taller than me.
　　　　　　　 "You fool" leaves were crumpled up. But I feel there won't be any difference.
8. Looking at the cross section of the stems through a microscope. (The illustration above)

「ありがとう」と呼びかけたヒマワリの根っこ
The roots of the sunflower that have been told "Thank you"

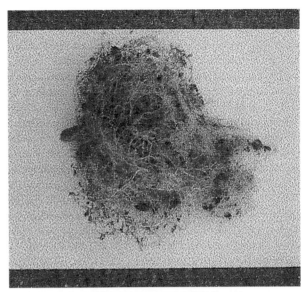

「ばかやろう」と呼びかけたヒマワリの根っこ
The roots of the sunflower that have been told "You fool"

おかあさん（足立敦子さん）の手紙から

子どもが送った手紙にお返事をくださり、本当にありがとうございました。

水の結晶写真に家族みんなが驚き、衝撃を受けました。夏休みの研究で子どもがヒマワリを育てました。毎日の水やり、観察と少々大変でしたが、なんとか結果を出すことができました。ありがとうございました。

途中まで江本さんのアドバイスの声かけをしましたが、子どものことです。「なんとなく、ばかやろうのヒマワリがかわいそうになってきて……。枯れることなく無事に花が咲いてほしい」と願うようになっていました。なかなか差がつかず困っていたところ、茎の切断面を顕微鏡でのぞいてみました。すると、「ありがとう」の茎の中の繊維は細かいつぶつぶ（繊維がぎっしりとつまっている）、「ばかやろう」は大きな変形したつぶ（繊維との間に隙間がありました）でした。

また根を見て驚きました。こんなに違いが出て、はっきり言ってびっくりです。

私は、これが「子育て」だったらどうなるんだろう……と怖い気がしました。

From her mum's letter (Atsuko Adachi)

Thank you very much for replying to my child's letter.

Our whole familiy was astonished and got a shock from the crystal photos of water.

My child grew sunflowers for the summer holiday assignment. It was a little burdensome for her to water them every day and observe them but somehow she was able to get results. Thank you.

Until a certain point, she took your advice, Mr. Emoto and talked to the plants. But since she is a child she started to wish "I don't know why, but I feel sorry for the "You fool" sunflowers....... I want them to flower without dying." She was troubled because there wasn't much difference in them, and at that point, we checked the cross section of the stems through a microscope. Then we found that the inside fibres of the "Thank you" stem were tightly filled with fine lumps (the fibres were packed tightly) and the "You fool" stem had big deformed lumps (there were spaces between the fibres).

We were also shocked to see the roots. There was such a difference between them, definitely. To be frank, it was shocking.

I was wondering if this had been a case of 'raising children', what would have happened.......I was scared.

「ありがとう」「ばかやろう」そして「無視」

ご飯の実験に、全国2カ所から、「無視」したというビンを加えたものが研究所に届けられています（月刊「波動」より）。これは、非常に興味深いものです。

1）読者の小針美保子さんの小学校5年生の息子さん、良友くんの実験では、「ありがとう」と「ばかやろう」の他に「なにも書かないビン」を合計3つ用意して、実験に取りかかりました。その結果、一番最初に腐り始め、ぐちゃぐちゃになったのは「なにも書かないビン」で、次が「ばかやろう」。「ありがとう」は、一部が黄色っぽくなったものの、急激な変化は見られなかったそうです。

2）同じ時期に、松本百代さん（主婦）がまったく同じ方法でおこなった結果をビデオで知らせてくれました。

結果はどちらも同じこと。

そしてなんと、良友くんも、松本さんも「なにも書かない」「何もしない」ということは、「無視」をすると同じことだという解釈をされていました。
ここにも非常に重要で新鮮な『水からの伝言・1』がありました。人に面と向かって悪口を言うと、確かに相手を傷つけます。しかし言う以上に相手を傷つけるのは「無視」するということ。「無視する」「シカトする」、腹立ちまぎれに何げなく……ということの怖さが身にしみますね。

"Thank you" "You fool" and "Ignoring"

To this experiment, glass containers, which had been "ignored" were added, and the results of that were sent from two areas around Japan to our Research Institute. (from the monthly magazine "HADO")

This is very interesting:

1. A boy called Yoshitomo in the 5th grade of an elementary school, is the magazine reader Mrs. Mihoko Kobari's son.

His experiment was:

All together there were three containers. Besides "Thank you" and "You fool", one with nothing written on it was prepared and we started the experiment. As a result, the first to get rotten and sloppy was the container with nothing written on it, and the second, "You fool".

"Thank you" didn't show any radical change but partially turned yellowish.

2. Around the same time, Mrs. Momoyo Matsumoto (housewife) experimented using exactly the same method and reported the result to us by a video.

Both results were the same.

On top of that, both Yoshitomo and Mrs. Matsumoto had the same understanding that "Nothing written on it" or "Doing nothing" is the same as "Ignoring". Here, we find a very important and refreshing "The Message from Water 1". When you speak ill of somebody in front of them, you definitely hurt them. However, this experiment shows us "Ignoring" can harm more than confronting.

"Ignoring" or "I've nothing more to say" spoken with anger, without thinking.....we can feel the fear of these in our bones .

世界を変えるのは私たちの心です！

ロサンゼルスより電子メール　岸　伸一さん

今、毎日レストランのお客様に、私の「ありがとう」と「ばかやろう」のご飯の実験の結果を見せて、『水からの伝言・1』の本を見せながら、説明して英語版のニュースレターを渡しています。皆さん大変に驚き、感動されるようです。

一人でも多くの人に、美しい心を持つことの重要性を、強く認識してもらいたい。それを伝え続けることで、より平和な世界に、より多くの人に本物の幸せになってもらえるなら、との思いからです。

東京都　江原弥生 先生

前略

5年2組ではこの1年間、みんなでいろいろなことを考え、クラスを（大きくは世界を）よりよくしていくためにどうしたらいいか、話し合ってきました。『水からの伝言・1』で出会った「ありがとう」という言葉の力（パワー）、環境問題への取り組み。その結果、とてもあたたかい集団をつくりあげていくことができました。クラスみんなの力です。

「自分がしてほしいことは、人にも同じようにしよう」この気持ちが、好意を示してくれた相手だけでなく、他の人々にも広げていけたら、本当に、確実に、世界は変わります。

世界を変えるのは私たちの心なのです。

Our mind is what changes the world !

An e-mail from Shinichi Kishi in Los Angeles

"These days I daily show my restaurant's customers the result of my rice experiment with "Thank you" and "You fool", and explain it to them with the book "The Message from Water 1". Then I give them a copy of our English newsletter. Everybody seems greatly amazed and impressed by it. I would like as many people as possible to be aware of the importance of keeping the mind beautiful. My reason for that is to create an even more peaceful world and an even greater number of people experiencing true happiness."

From Yayoi Ehara, a school teacher in Tokyo city

In class 2 of the 5th grade, throughout this year, we have pondered upon many things together and we have discussed with each other what to do to make our class (on a larger scale, our world) better...We came across the powerful word "Thank you" and also learned how to take part in the environmental problem, in "The Message from Water 1". The result was that we were able to create a very warm group. That is because of the efforts of all the members of the class.

"Let's do unto others as we would have others do unto us." If we could spread this feeling to many other people, not just to those who were good to you, this world wouldl definitely change.

Our mind is what changes the world !

寒い冷蔵庫の中での楽しみ！

IHM総合研究所　主任研究員　木津孝誠

結晶撮影スタッフになる以前は、私も一読者として「水からの伝言」の結晶写真の魅力にとりつかれていました。でも写真を通じて知っていた結晶の表情は、今考えるとほんの一コマに過ぎませんでした。顕微鏡から観察する結晶は写真以上に美しく非常に神秘的です。つくづく皆さんにも直接顕微鏡からの映像をお見せしたいと思うばかりです。

そこで、読者の皆さんの想像力を頼りに、皆さんも撮影者の目になって一緒に冷蔵庫に入っていただくことにしましょう。

まず、防寒着に身を包み、マイナス５度に設定された大型冷蔵庫のドアを開けます。そこには水を氷結させる冷凍庫と、台に置かれた光学顕微鏡。その中間に撮影者が座る椅子があります。撮影環境はそこに「もぐり込む」という表現がぴったりです。バタンと冷蔵庫のドアを閉め、椅子に座ると聞こえてくるのは冷蔵庫のモーター音だけ。さあ、冷凍庫から出番を待っているシャーレを取り出します。

蓋を取ったシャーレの上の氷塊を、横から見るとツンと立った突起があるのがわかります。結晶はその突起の頂上にあるのです。まるで植物が成長して先端に花をつけるように、隆起した氷の頂点に水の華が開いています。まったく不思議ですね。

顕微鏡の光は上から落射されています。すばやく光の下に突起の頂点をもっていきます。ここはなるべくスピーディにしましょう。冷凍庫と冷蔵庫の温度差によって、氷が溶けはじめます。溶けはじめると固定していたものが、急に動き始め、結晶が成長することになります。すでに結晶の成長は始まっています。

さあ、いよいよ結晶とのご対面。接眼レンズを覗き込むと、まだピントの合っていない結晶は、ぼんやりとした光の集合体に見えます。薄曇りの満月の夜に雲を通して漏れる、ほのかな光のようです。そこに雲を突き抜けるようにピントを合わせると、満月ならぬ六角形の結晶がポコンと現れます。

Having fun in the cold refrigerator !

by Takashige Kizu, chief researcher at the I.H.M. General Research Institute

Even before I became a staff member taking crystal photographs I was, as one reader of "The Message from Water", totally engrossed in the photographs of those crystals. However, the 'expression' of the crystals I came to know through the photographs was nothing more than a single frame. The crystals I observed directly through the microscope were more beautiful than the photographs and mysterious.

I would very much like to show you those images directly revealed through the microscope.

Therefore, I would also like you to have the eye of the photographer and thus, trusting in the reader"s imagination, enter the refrigerated room together.

First of all, we shall don our arctic clothes and open the door of a huge room set at -5℃ . There sits a freezer which freezes the water and an optical microscope placed on a stand. In between these, there is a chair for the photographer to sit on.

The expression 'squeezes into' best describes the scene of entering this photographic environment. Once you shut the refrigerator door and sit on that chair, only the sound of the refrigerator's motor can be heard. Now, let's take out the petri dish which finds itself waiting first in line inside the freezer.

Observing the lump of ice on the petri dish from the side, after taking off the cover, you will find a protruberance. It is on the tip of that protruberance where you will find the crystal. As if a plant had grown to bloom at its extremities, we found a water 'flower' opening on the tip of the protruding ice. It is utterly mysterious.

The light of the microscope is shining downward from above. You rapidly position the apex of the protruberance under this light. Let's try to do this as speedily as possible. It will start to melt because of the difference in temperature betweeen the freezer and the refrigerated room.

As soon as it starts melting, what is fixed suddenly starts to move and this causes the growth of the crystal. The growth of the crystal has already started .

At last, the encounter happens between you and the crystal. When you look through the ocular lense, the crystal which is not yet in clear focus looks like a vague amalgamation of light. It appears like the faint light which can be seen leaking through the clouds

結晶の一生は数十秒です。核の周辺にある飾りがその間にどんどん成長し、光の乱反射によって、まばゆいばかりに輝き出します。六方向に広がる枝葉は、そう、まさに葉っぱや花弁のように成長していきます。まるで成長するダイヤモンドです。

それは溜息の出る美しさ……！ でも見惚れている時間はありません。目を接眼レンズからカメラのファインダーへと移動させ、決定的瞬間を撮影です。「パシャリ、パシャリ」。撮影の最中にも結晶はフレームに収まりきれないくらい、どんどん伸びていきます。

そしてたとえばここでピントをわずかに動かしてみると、結晶は核を中心にして立体的に成長していくのがわかります。花にたとえると、コスモスのように核と花弁が平面に近い結晶もあれば、薔薇や菊の花のように核が奥まった、立体感のある結晶もあります。

200倍の倍率の世界ですから、微妙な高さの違いは、結晶の核と枝葉、両者にピントを均一に合わせられないほどです。写真にある様々な結晶を見て、その立体感を想像していただけるでしょうか。

そして冷凍庫から取り出して数10秒後。誕生から休むことなく成長を続けた結晶が、ピタリと止まって見える時があります。結晶の成長が終わって、水へと変わる瞬間です。結晶はまったく静止することなく今度は水になろうとするのです。それは水の分子が絶えず動き回っているという事実を思い出させてくれます。

ぼんやりと結晶の美しい表情を撮れた安堵感に浸っていると、冷蔵庫のモーター音が再び聞こえてきます。そして再び次のシャーレを冷凍庫から取り出す……というのが撮影の流れです。

いかがでしょう。結晶写真はわずか数10秒間という、結晶のドラマチックな一生のワンショットなのです。

on a full moon night. Then you get it in focus and it's just like the light has pierced through the clouds. It is not the full moon though, but a hexagonal crystal which effortlessly appears!

The life of the crystal is a few score seconds. The decorative part around the nucleus starts to grow progressively faster during this interval and it starts to shine dazzlingly due to the diffused reflection of light. Its branching leaves spread into six directions, and just like leaves or flowers, it grows. It looks as if a diamond were growing.

This is indeed mesmerizingly beautiful! But you don't have time to lose yourself in watching. You move your eyes from the eyepiece of the microscope to the finder of the camera and shoot this crucial moment. "Click, click." Even while taking the picture, the crystal stretches outward further, so that it can no longer fit inside the frame.

Furthermore, if you try to adjust the focus even slightly, you will find the crystal growing three-dimensionally centred around the nucleus. If we compare this to flowers, the nucleus and petals of the cosmos are close to being a flat level crystal while on the other hand flowers like roses and chrysanthemums have a deep nucleus and a stereographic feel as crystals.

Because this is a world of two hundred times magnification, subtle differences in height make the crystals' branches and leaves hard to equally focus on. Try to imagine that three dimensionality when looking at the various crystals in the photographs.

A score of seconds after being taken out of the freezer, there is a moment when the ever growing crystal, which has not rested since its inception, seems to suddenly stop. This is the instant when the crystal's growth melts to change into water. Completely without stopping, next it starts changing into water. This seems to remind us of the fact that the water's molecules are ceaselessly in motion.

Just as you sink into that fuzzy feeling of ease that you have captured the beautiful expression of the crystal you hear the sound of the freezer's motor. And then, it's on to taking out the next petri dish in line.... this is how the flow of our photography continues.

So how about it? This is how one shot of a crystal in the seconds of its dramatic life unfolds!

結晶写真・撮影記録について

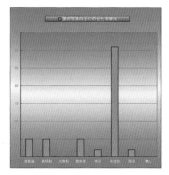

IHM総合研究所
IHM General Research Institute

私たちは撮影ごとに、結晶のでき方をグラフにして保存しています。たとえば、本著89ページでご紹介した「蓮の花の写真を見せた蒸留水」の結晶の場合、左のようなグラフになります。

グラフは左から、美結晶、美傾斜、六角形、放射状、格子、不定形、陥没、結晶なし……と別れています。一番多く現れた不定形の結晶の中から江本会長がもっとも美しいと感じた3枚です。ちなみに下の12枚も、同じ時に撮影した50枚のうちの一部です。

About how we keep a record of the crystal photographs
Each time we photograph the water crystals we make and keep a graph of how the crystals form. For example, when we showed distilled water a photograph of a lotus flower as introduced on page 89 of this book, the graph taken looks like the one on the left. From the left side of the graph, beautiful crystals, aesthetic inclination, hexagon, radiating, lattice, uncertain formation, depression, and non crystalization. These three shots are the ones Mr. Emoto felt were the most beautiful. By the way, the twelve shots below are part of fifty that were taken at the same time.

あ とがき

江本　勝

皆さん、『水からの伝言・2』お楽しみ頂けましたでしょうか。

面白いもので著者としてみれば、やはり2冊目という余裕でしょうか、案外楽しみながらこの本をまとめることができました。きっとその波動を皆さんも感じられたことと思います。

それにしてもお水さんのメッセージはすごいものがありますね。きっとそうに違いないと考え、この方法を編み出した当人である私でさえ、びっくりすることの連続です。たとえば10ページの『夫婦愛』、まさかこのような形で具体的に見せてくれるとは、本当にびっくりし、感動させられました。

そして極め付きは23ページの『競争』です。私としてはてっきり美しい結晶は撮れないであろうと予測していました。しかしごらんのように凛々とした美しい結晶となりました。これはどういう事だろうと、ちょっと焦りながら考えてみました。"えーと、美しい結晶が撮れたということはこの言葉は大自然の摂理にかなっているというわけだから、あっ、そうか『競争』ということは大自然にとってはごく当たり前のことなんだ。みんなより強い子孫を作るべく一生懸命、いろいろと工夫しているし、自分自身も成長するために、ほかの仲間や、ライバルに負けないように必死にがんばって努力しているもんなあ。ということは人間社会でも競争は、理にかなっていることなんだ……"と教えられたのです。

他にも私が新たに教えられたり、気付かされたり、再確認させられたことはたくさんありました。今までの私の考えが間違っていたということもありました。とにかくお水さんの教えは、私にとっては脱帽することばかりです。しかしそれはあくまでも私の印象であり、押し付けられるべきものではありません。それは第1集の"しようね""しなさい"という言葉の結晶の違いによく表れています。

ですから皆さんがどう感じ、どう思われるかが大切で、そしてその集約されたものが世論をつくり、明日の社会を築いてゆくのだと思います。

皆さま、この写真集は何度も何度も時間がおありのとき、そして何か悲しいこと、楽しいことがあったときにそのつどページを開いてみてください。おそらくその折ごとに、感じられ方が違ってくると思います。それが定まるようになれば、あなたの感性、すなわち右脳は、もう一歩ステップアップされるのではないかと、僭越ながら私は思います。

おしまいになりましたが、この『水からの伝言・2』についても私の意図するところを十分に、いやそれ以上に汲み取っていただきすばらしい編集をしてくださったなるかげつねこさんをはじめとする（株）サンクリエートのみなさま、『水からの伝言・1』に引き続き見事な風景写真を提供してくださった川崎徳次郎さん、そして寒い冷蔵室の中で精力的に美しい写真を撮り続けてくれた木津孝誠君をはじめとする新旧I.H.Mのスタッフ諸君、さらに、翻訳を担当してくれた愛知ソニアさん、それを補佐してくれた旦那さまのエハン・デラヴィさん、みなみなさま本当にありがとうございました。心より愛と感謝の思いをささげます。

2001年9月10日

補記

全ての原稿を書き上げ、編集の最終打ち合わせのために訪れた神戸のサンクリエート社で、今この補記を書いています。9月11日、世界中を震撼させたあの恐ろしいテロ事件が発生してしまいました。21世紀になって何か大変なことが起こるであろうと私は予測していましたが、まさかこ

のような形でそれが起こるとは想像だにできないことでありました。今となってはこのことが新たなる殺戮を生み出さないよう祈るばかりですが、それもかなり難しいこととなるのでしょう。

　この悲劇を生み出した大きな要因のひとつは、長い長い歴史の中で宿命的に誕生してしまった民族間の宗教の違いによる相克であるのは、誰もが理解をしていることです。ふつう原因がわかっていれば、その対処方法も自ら得ることができるものですが、この宗教観の違いによる争いについては、もうかれこれ、それが始まってから３千年はたつというのに、いまだに誰もその方法を、知恵を編み出しえていません。

　本来は同じ根源であるはずのそれぞれの宗教が、なぜこのようにこんがらがってしまったのか、私はそれらを解く鍵として、人類共通のテーマである生命の原点に今一度みんなで立ち返ってこれを考えていくことしか他に方法はないと考えます。それも誰にでも解りやすい方法で。

　生命の原点、それは物質的に言えば水です。そして今までその水のことは、科学的に見ても不可解なものとされてきました。ですから水についての解釈は人によって、地域によって、そして時によって、諸説入り乱れる解釈の歴史ともなっています。ですから生命の根源を説く宗教もまた、諸説あるものとなってしまったのだと私は考えています。

　今ここに、それらの要求を満たすものが誕生しました。それがこの『水からの伝言』です。ぜひこの本を世界中の友、とくにそれぞれの宗教を信ずる友に見せていただくよう、著者として心よりお願い申し上げます。

　これは、緊急発信です。

Afterword
by Masaru Emoto

　Have you enjoyed the second collection of "The Message from Water"? It is interesting that, perhaps due to this being the second book and my having a little leeway, I had a surprisingly good time in compiling it. Undoubtedly you, the reader also felt that HADO, I believe .

　That being said, the message from our water has something amazing, doesn't it? I think that is surely the case, moreso by being the one who devised this method and being continuously amazed by it. For example, take the "Love of husband and wife" on page10. I was truly astonished and moved by that unexpectedly concrete form it expressed.

　Next, there was the widely acknowledged "competition" crystal on page23. I was dead sure in my estimation that it would never get a beautiful crystal but as you can see, it became an awe inspiringly beautiful one. With some impatience, I wondered what this could possibly mean. "Well then, here we have a beautiful crystal and this word "competition" obeys the providence of nature and so, yes, that's it, from nature's point of view, war is a totally commonplace thing, to create stronger descendants with all one's might, to make efforts in various ways, in order to survive.

Of course, you would do your best to not be beaten by friend or enemy. That is to say, even in human society, competition stands to reason." This is what it taught me.

Besides that, I was taught anew, was awakened and had many things reconfirmed. I also realized that I had been mistaken in some of my thinking until now. In any case, the teaching from water was for me a continual action of taking off of my hat to it. However, that was strictly my own impression and is not something to be forced upon others. In volume 1, this is well expressed in the crystals for "Let's Do It" and "Do It".

I think what is important therefore is how you, the readers, think and feel. Then the intensification of that will create a public consensus which goes on to build tomorrow's society.

Whenever you have time please open these pages. When something sad or something happy happens, each time, again and again open them. I think that perhaps each time you do, you will feel something different. Whilst it may be presumptuous of me, I think that when those thoughts and feelings become definite, your sensitivity, that is your right brain, will have made another step forward.

In conclusion, I would like to express my thanks to the following people for making allowances above and beyond the intentions I had for this second collection, beginning with Tsuneko Narukage who edited this book fabulously and all the staff of Sun Create Inc. and Mr. Tokujiro Kawasaki for the outstanding landscape photographs he has provided continuously since "The Message from Water 1". Then starting with Mr. Takashige Kizu, who continued to take beautiful photographs in the cold refrigerated room with such zest, all of the new and old staff of IHM company, and further Sonia Aichi who was in charge of translation and her husband Echan Deravy who assisted her, thank you all so very much. From the bottom of my heart, I offer you thoughts of love and gratitude.

September 10th, 2001

Postscript

I am writing this postscript in the Kobe office of Sun Create Inc., having completed the writing of the manuscript. I have come here for the final briefing with my editor. It is September 11th and the whole world has just been shaken by the outbreak of that terrorist event. Although I had felt that something incredible would happen in the 21st century, I could never have imagined it occuring in this fashion. Now that it has come to this, I am just praying that it will not give birth to further massacre, but that is also going to be very difficult.

What has given rise to this tragedy is something that anybody can understand. It is that rivalry between the religions of different ethnic groups, fatefully given birth to over long, long ages. Normally if one knows the cause, a method of dealing with the problem can be found by oneself. However, when it comes to the case of different religious viewpoints, more or less three thousand years have already passed since then, with still nobody having been able to devise the wisdom or the way.

How did the different religions, which must have originally had the same source, become so entangled? I believe there is a key to unravelling this in a common theme of humanity which, for all of us now harks back to the source of life. I believe there is no other way forward for us but this.

It is a way that anyone can easily understand. The source of life, if you were to put it in words as something material, is water. And until now that water has been something inexplicable, even when looked at scientifically. Therefore, when it comes to our understanding of water, depending on the people, the Earth and the time, it has been a history of one confusion after another amongst the various theories. That is why I think it will be the same case too, of various confusing theories, with any religion that unravels the source of life.

Here and now however, something that fulfills those needs has been born. It is "The Message from Water". As the author, I respectfully suggest from the bottom of my heart that you show this book to friends all over the world, especially friends of each and every religious belief.

This is an urgent message.

著者　江本 勝（えもと　まさる）

1943年7月横浜市に生まれる。横浜市立大学文理学部国際関係論学科を卒業。
（株）地産、中部読売新聞社（現、読売新聞中部本社）などを経て、1986年、株式会社 I.H.M.を設立。
1992年10月に『オープン・インターナショナル・ユニバーシティー』より、代替医療学の認定を受け、ライセンスを交付される。アメリカで共鳴磁場分析器やマイクロクラスター水に出会い、水の謎に挑む。
科学の目というよりも、人間としてのオリジナルな視点で、身体の中の水、身の回りの水、地球上の水の研究にとり組んでいる。ついに、水のもつ本来の自然な姿が、その結晶から判明することに気づき、ユニークな実験を続けている。
現在、I.H.M.総合研究所所長、（株）I.H.M.代表取締役、（株）I.H.M.国際波動友の会代表。
著書『波動時代への序幕』（サンロード出版）など多数。

訳者　愛知ソニア

日本に生まれ、英国に渡り美術を専攻する。日本でエハン・デラヴィと結婚し、三児の母親となる。その時期に子育ての合間に禅、マクロビオティック、ヨガを学び、12年前に家族とカナダに移住した。「マージング・ポイント」（1993年、日本で出版）を夫と共著。日本語翻訳本に次のものがある。「光の家族」（太陽出版）、「インディゴ・チルドレン」（ナチュラルスピリット）。現在、大阪に在住。

About the author

Masaru Emoto was born in Yokohama in July 1943. He graduated from the International Relations course in the Department of Humanities and Sciences at Yokohama Municipal University. In 1986 he established the I.H.M. Corporation having previously had experience with the Chisan company and the Chubu Yomiuri Newspaper (now the Yomiuri Shinbun Chubu main office). In October of 1992 he received certification from the Open International University, thus becoming licensed in the field of Alternative Medicine. In America he was introduced to micro-cluster water as well as magnetic resonance analysis technology. Here began the challenge of the mystery of water.

He undertook research of Earth's water, of the water around us and in our bodies, not so much with a scientific eye as from an original perspective,as a human being. At length he realized that the original, natural form that water has is confirmed through the crystals. He continues with his unique experimentation. He is currently the head of the I.H.M. General Research Institute Inc., the President of I.H.M. Inc. and the chief representative of I.H.M's International HADO Fellowship. His many published works include "Prelude to the HADO Age" from Sun Road Publishing.

About the translator

Sonia Aichi was born in Japan and studied art in the U.K. She married Echan Deravy in Japan and became the mother of three children. During her years parenting she studied Zen, Macrobiotic cooking and Yoga before moving with the family to Canada 12 years ago. She co-authored the book "Merging Point" (published in Japanese in 1993) with her husband and has translated into Japanese the following books: Family of Light (Bear and Co.) and Indigo Children (Hay House Inc.) She currently lives in Osaka, Japan.

参考にさせていただきました／Many thanks for these references

- NHK ビデオ「生命」／NHK video "LIFE"
- ホームクラシック名曲集／Home Classic Masterpieces
- EMI CLASSICS／EMI Classics／Wagner Orchestral Works
- ワグナー管弦楽曲集／Violin Concerto "Il Cimento Dell'armonia e dell'inventione"
- バイオリン協奏曲集「和声と創意への試み」／Albinoni Concerto
- アルビノーニ協奏曲集／Albinoni Concerto
- The Amazing Bud Powell／The Amazing Bud Powell
- 宇多田ヒカル「Automatic」／"Automatic" by Hikaru Utada
- バリ島呪的合唱曲「神々の森のケチャ」／"The Choral Drama of Singapadu Village "Kecak"
- オリジナル サウンドトラック「サウンドオブミュージック」／Original Sound Track "The Sound of Music"
- 世界愛唱名曲アルバム／World Favourites Masterpiece Album
- 日本のしらべ／Japanese Tunes
- キングレコード「落語」CD／King Records "Rakugo" CD
- 日本の民謡／Japanese Folk Songs
- 日本の民謡大百科／The encyclopedia of Japanese Folk Songs
- 環境音楽／Environmental Music

水からの伝言 Vol.2
今日も水にありがとう

発 行 日……2001年 11月15日第1版 第1刷発行
　　　　　　2002年 1月30日第1版 第3刷発行
編 著 者……江本 勝
撮　　　影……I.H.M総合研究所
　　　　　　木津 孝誠　押手 孝行　勝亦 健　小松 彰良
　　　　　　佐藤 誠哉　田中 みぎわ　二村 潤
発 行 者……(株) 波動教育社
　　　　　　〒111-0052　東京都台東区柳橋2-14-4
　　　　　　ワグナービル2F
　　　　　　電話 03-3866-3592
発 売 元……(株) I.H.M.
　　　　　　〒111-0052　東京都台東区柳橋2-14-4
　　　　　　ワグナービル2F
　　　　　　電話 03-3866-3713
　　　　　　Fax 03-3866-3763
　　　　　　http://www.hado.com
ヨーロッパ連絡事務所……Hado Publishing B.V.
　　　　　　Duivendrechtsekade 42,
　　　　　　1096AH, Amsterdam,
　　　　　　The Netherlands
　　　　　　電話 31-20-4629-640
　　　　　　Fax 31-20-4629-729
　　　　　　book@hado.net
　　　　　　www.hado.net
翻　　　訳……愛知ソニア
編　　　集……(株) サンクリエート
写 真 提 供……川崎 徳二郎
製版・印刷……株式会社ワイ・エスカラー
定　　　価……2,700円+税
　　　　　　落丁・乱丁本はお取り替えいたします
　　　　　　※記事、写真などの転載についてはご一報ください

The Message from Water vol.2
thank you again today, water
First issue, First edition, November 15, 2001
Third issue, First edition, January 30, 2002
　　Edited by Masaru Emoto
Photographed by I.H.M. General Research Institute
Takashige Kizu Takayuki Oshide Takeshi Katsumata
Akiyoshi Komatsu Masaya Sato Migiwa Tanaka
Jun Futamura
Published by HADO Kyoikusha
2F, Wagner Bldg. 2-14-4, Yanagibashi, Taito-ku, Tokyo,
111-0052 JAPAN
Tel: 81-3-3866-3713
Sold by I.H.M. Co., Ltd.
2F, Wagner Bldg. 2-14-4, Yanagibashi, Taito-ku, Tokyo,
111-0052 JAPAN
Tel: 81-3-3866-3713/Fax:81-3-3866-3763
Hado Publishing B.V.
European office, Duivendrechtsekade 42,
1096AH, Amsterdam, The Netherlands
Tel:31-20-4629-640
Fax:31-20-4629-729
book@hado.net
www.hado.net
Translated by Sonia Aichi
Compiled by Sun Create K.K.
Photos provided by Tokujiro Kawasaki
Typeset and printed by K.K. YS Colour
Price:￥2,700+tax
Exchangeable in case of missing pages and/or incorrect
collation.
Please inform us before reproducing any articles
and pictures.